Antique French Jewelry
1800–1950

This book was published with the support of
the Institut National de Gemmologie and Maison Riondet

Editorial partnerships
Henri Julien and Emmanuelle Rolland

Editorial director
Kate Mascaro

Editor (French edition)
Virginie Maubourguet

Editor (English edition)
Helen Adedotun

Translation from the French
Alexandra Keens

Graphic design and typesetting
Nolwen Lauzanne

Copyediting
Lindsay Porter

Proofreading
Nicole Foster

Production
Louisa Hanifi-Morard

Color separation
IGS-CP L'Isle d'Espagnac

Printed in Slovenia by Florjancic

Originally published in French as *Bijoux anciens,
1800-1950: Découvrir, identifier et apprécier*
© Flammarion, S.A., Paris, 2021

English-language edition
© Éditions Flammarion, Paris, 2024

editions.flammarion.com
@flammarioninternational
partenariats@flammarion.fr

24 25 26   3 2 1

ISBN: 978-2-08-043331-2

Legal Deposit: 03/2024

Editorial direction by
Geoffray Riondet

Foreword by
Victoire de Castellane

Antique
French 1800–1950
Jewelry

In collaboration with
Valérie Goupil
and
Anne Laurent
Brigitte Serre-Bouret
Loïc Lescuyer
Gérard Panczer

Flammarion

Contents

Plate 1 from *Le Bijou: Revue artistique et industrielle de la bijouterie, joaillerie, orfèvrerie, musée pratique à l'usage des joailliers, bijoutiers, orfèvres, estampeurs, graveurs, peintres*, J. Rothschild (ed.), 1878

Foreword

I have always liked to imagine jewelry as one vast family in which eighteenth-century parures are the great-great-great-grandparents of contemporary pieces, and the different periods can meet and mingle, exchange and live together. It's a family tree with ancient roots that stretch throughout the world in different directions, and every branch contains a universe of its own. Every period appeals to me; each one offers a stone, motif, or technique that I find fascinating. I like to wear these pieces in combination—they seem to recognize each other and to tell one another their family stories.

It was also antique jewelry that fostered my love of gems. When I was a child, and up until the late 1990s, I was all about the four precious stones: diamond, ruby, sapphire, and emerald. As I explored the antique shops and learned more about the history of jewelry, I discovered a whole wide world of gemstones. I was about fifteen years old and I learned their poetic names, their countless shades of color, and their origins. The anecdotes about them amused me: for example, the fact that the red stones in royal crowns, usually mistaken for rubies, are in fact very often spinels—the name alone enchanted me.

I have always recounted stories through the jewelry that I make. I want each creation to form a little narrative sculpture. Antique jewelry pieces are vessels for so many stories, and that is probably where my love for them comes from. First of all, there's the motif, of course, as is the case for any item of jewelry: a flower, an animal, an abstract geometric pattern. But these pieces also speak, more broadly, of an era: of social trends, of women's tastes, of stone-cutting or setting techniques. They reveal the work of the craftsperson and of their skillful hands. They convey incredible memories of the ages and civilizations. And then, added to all these interlocking stories, there is another layer of narrative, perhaps the most poetic of them all: that of the lives of the women who wore these jewels and loved them. Sometimes we know part of the story, when it is a historic piece or a family heirloom. But more often than not, we know nothing, and the jewelry alone remains to fuel our dreams and our imagination. And that's when everything becomes possible.

Victoire de Castellane

Preface

Jewelry has existed since the origins of humankind. It is found in every culture and in all human groups. Although the symbolic element of jewelry has gradually given way to its ornamental function, it still has a meaningful dimension, and in this respect it can provide many economic, social, and religious indicators.

This book is the first practical volume to offer a comprehensive overview of antique French jewelry, including all the useful information that readers need to know. The period that it covers—from the French Directory of the late eighteenth century to the 1950s—was a logical choice. Not only does the French Revolution (1789–1799) mark a turning point, but it is also extremely rare to find jewelry dating from before the eighteenth century on the market: besides the inevitable wear and tear, these antique works were often transformed to suit contemporary tastes. The nineteenth century and the first half of the twentieth century constituted a new era in the history of jewelry, as France regained its prestige. A succession of highly diverse styles combined traditional craftsmanship and a constant quest for innovation. Jewelry from this period often displays lost skills and remains a more or less conscious source of inspiration for contemporary designers.

Illustrated with drawings, photographs, and archival documents—often published for the first time—this simple yet complete guide offers aficionados a thorough understanding of antique French jewelry, while providing specialists with a useful reference tool.

Before embarking on this vast subject, it is helpful, perhaps, to examine the term "jewelry." The word "jewel" has been in use since the late thirteenth century, derived from the Anglo-French word, "juel" and the Old French "jouel," meaning ornament, gift, or gem. By the late fourteenth century, "juelrye" was used to refer to "precious ornaments" or "jewelwork." Some have also traced the word "jewel" to the Latin "jocale," a word which relates to games and jokes, or "that which causes joy."

Geoffray Riondet

Jewelry through Time

La Mode illustrée, no. 39, Sunday, September 27, 1868

Introduction

Since jewelry reflects its era, it is useful to consider the political and economic situation of each period. The nineteenth century and the first half of the twentieth century saw a succession of highly diverse styles, which wasn't the case in previous centuries. However, while a given style may be associated with a certain period, it will always have developed slowly over time, heralded by early signs and drawing on the past and on outside influences. Similarly, a style only disappears after a lengthy decline. Fashions usually coexist from one period to the next.

Jean-Auguste-Dominique Ingres, *Princesse de Broglie*, 1853

Parure, First Empire period •
gold, carnelian, natural pearls,
enamel, tortoiseshell

The Consulate and the First Empire (1799–1814)

Context

France had just experienced one of the most troubled periods of its history. The Revolution had had a huge impact on all of society. The old nobility found itself impoverished and most of its members in exile. The establishment of the Consulate and, to an even greater degree, the First Empire, brought a newfound freedom, and tastes were increasingly influenced by the bourgeoisie.

Under the impetus of Emperor Napoleon, the country regained its position as the epicenter of jewelry design. Challenges remained, however. The Revolution had brought an end to the

system of trade guilds. The profession was slowly reorganizing itself but struggled to meet demand because of the scarcity of raw materials. To solve this problem, the oldest jewelry pieces were taken apart and the gold and precious stones recycled. At the time, the British would say that there were three sources for diamonds: Southeast Asia, Brazil, and the French Revolution. And so it was that the skills of French jewelry makers came fully into their own.

Inspirations and Trends

Still rooted in neoclassicism, jewelry designs were influenced by antiquity.

Greece and Imperial Rome became the prime references. While the French Revolution profoundly transformed social structures and the art world, stylistic forms had moved on earlier. Interest in antiquity began in the mid-eighteenth century following recent archeological discoveries, especially the excavations in Herculaneum in 1738 and in Pompeii ten years later. Europe rediscovered these civilizations and idealized them.

Women's Greco-Roman-style clothing, notably long, loose dresses gathered under the bust, with narrow sleeves and a low-cut neckline, was particularly well suited to the wearing of jewelry.

Under the influence of antiquity, glyptics, or gemstone carving, in intaglio (cut into the background) or in relief (cameos), enjoyed unprecedented popularity. The carved figures were taken from mythology. To boost this new trend, Napoleon I created a school within the Institution Impériale des Sourds-Muets (School for the Deaf and Dumb) in Paris, and founded a "grand prix" in 1805. The *Journal des dames et des modes* dated 25 Ventôse, year XIII (March 16, 1805) mentions the trend: "A fashionable woman wears cameos at her belt, cameos on her collar, a cameo on each of her bracelets, a cameo on her tiara; on her Greco-Roman chair are cameos."

The same period saw the emergence of Egyptology, with the French campaign in Egypt (1798–1801). Dominique Vivant Denon's book *Voyage dans la Basse et la Haute Égypte* (*Travels in Upper and Lower Egypt*), published in 1802, became a source of inspiration. Women wore jewelry inspired by ancient Egypt, with sphinx and pyramid motifs. The scarab beetle, a symbol of resurrection, was also popular. For his Polish mistress, Marie Walewska, Napoleon had a ring mounted with a pivoting scarab, fashioned out of a fragment of the cannon ball that killed his horse at the Battle of Dresden on August 26, 1813, with the place and date inscribed on the back.

Portrait medallion depicting Empress Joséphine • gold, miniature on ivory, natural pearls, hair

Necklace, c. 1830 • gold, citrine

The Restoration (1814–1830) and the July Monarchy (1830–1848)

Context

After the fall of the First Empire, the Bourbons returned to power with the Count of Provence, who reigned as Louis XVIII from 1815 to 1824, followed by the Count of Artois, known as Charles X, from 1824 to 1830. These two monarchs sought to restore the ancien régime, as France was experiencing significant economic difficulties following Napoleon's many campaigns.

In 1830, the July Revolution saw the overthrow of Charles X. Constitutional monarchy was retained at the price of a change of dynasty. Louis Philippe I was proclaimed King of the French. His reign was characterized by the development of the financial and manufacturing bourgeoisie and their rapid accumulation of wealth. His peaceful life at the Tuileries Palace reflected the aspirations of the bourgeoisie of his time, but the economic crisis that hit the country from 1846 followed by the Revolution of 1848 hindered the creative sector.

Inspirations and Trends

Romanticism, which had appeared in the late eighteenth century in Germany, England, and France, lasted until the Second Empire. Nostalgia greatly influenced jewelry design. The *Petit Courrier des dames* (1829) noted that "hair styles, laden with a mass of different ornaments, were like whole museums in themselves, combining all the jewelry that art and coquetry had invented over the years."

While antiquity remained the main source of inspiration until 1820, the idealized Middle Ages gave rise to the neo-Gothic or "cathedral" style. The success of Victor Hugo's novel *Notre-Dame de Paris* (*The Hunchback of Notre-Dame*), published in 1831, and the historical drama *La Tour de Nesle* (*The Tower of Nesle*) by Frédéric Gaillardet and Alexandre Dumas, published the following year, popularized the medieval style. The jewelry maker François-Désiré Froment-Meurice largely contributed to this trend; Victor Hugo dedicated a poem to him in his *Contemplations* of 1841.

Meanwhile, the neo-Renaissance style was slowly emerging. Some jewelers drew inspiration from the few fifteenth- and sixteenth-century pieces displayed at the Louvre or the Cabinet des Médailles. Others were inspired by paintings, such as Leonardo da Vinci's *La Belle Ferronnière*, a three-quarter portrait of a woman wearing a head ornament. This type of piece, often consisting of a chain with a gold motif or stone or pearl on the forehead, was very fashionable from 1820. As in the Renaissance, jewelry featured cameos and pearls, often baroque and mounted in a pendant or drops. The royal court initiated this fashion, which was followed by a wider, bourgeois clientele. These pieces proved highly popular under the July Monarchy, coming back into fashion in the Second Empire.

From 1820, naturalistic motifs in the eighteenth-century tradition gradually reappeared, with jewelry favoring animal, bird, or floral themes. Flowers in countless

Bracelet by François-Désiré Froment-Meurice (goldsmith), James Pradier (sculptor), Jules Wièse (maker), 1841 • silver, enamel, ruby, pearl

variations were dotted over the hair, décolletages, bodices, and belts. In 1820, on the occasion of the birth of the Duke of Bordeaux, the Duchess of Berry was presented with an ornament featuring a large floral bouquet tied with a ribbon, made by the Bapst jewelry house. This theme was in vogue from 1820 to 1860. Certain motifs, such as flowers and insects, were mounted on a spring so as to tremble at the slightest movement, in a bid to make them look as natural as possible.

Exoticism was another major source of inspiration. The French conquest of Algeria in 1830 led to "Moorish" jewelry. The *Revue des modes de Paris* noted the trend the same year: "The taking of Algiers is not only the topic of salons, it's in all the shops. It comes in the form of crescent-moon earrings and parures called 'algériennes.'" When the Luxor Obelisk was erected on Place de la Concorde in Paris in 1836, it revived the Egyptian fashion sparked by the campaign of 1798. Scarab beetles and hieroglyphs would remain popular motifs throughout the nineteenth century.

Jewelry was not only worn by women. Dandyism, which started in London in the early nineteenth century, spread to Paris from 1825. For aficionados of the style, their appearance became their main occupation. In his *Illusions perdues*, published in 1836 to 1843, Honoré de Balzac summed up men's fashion under the July Monarchy in his description of Lucien de Rubempré: "Lucien had wonderful canes, and a charming eyeglass; he had diamond studs, and scarf-rings, and signet-rings, besides an assortment of waistcoats marvelous to behold, and in sufficient number to match every color in a variety of costumes." Men's jewelry consisted principally of rings, tie pins, and watch chains.

Jean-Baptiste Paulin Guérin, *Marie-Caroline, Princess of Bourbon-Two Sicilies, Duchess of Berry*, 1816

"En Tremblant" (trembling) • brooch, late nineteenth century silver and gold, diamonds

The Second Empire (1852–1870)

Context

The Second Empire was a period of rapid expansion, with a growing economy supported by the banks. Increasing industrialization put luxury goods, including jewelry, within the reach of a larger section of the population. The Paris World's Fairs (Expositions Universelles) of 1855 and 1867 stimulated activity in the economic, artistic, and cultural spheres, while the country's figureheads, Napoleon III and Empress Eugénie, set the tone in many areas.

Inspirations and Trends

There was such enthusiasm for all things new during this period that the Second Empire is largely characterized by the diversity of its inspirations. Jewelry was not homogeneous in style, and eclecticism prevailed during the reign of Napoleon III. An admirer of Marie Antoinette, Empress Eugénie fostered a revival of seventeenth-century French art. Decorative motifs of the Louis XV and Louis XVI eras, notably featuring bows, came back into fashion. The Bapst jewelry house remounted some of the French Crown jewels in the style of the seventeenth century.

A new taste for antiquity was spawned by the Campana collection, acquired in 1860 by Napoleon III after hard negotiations. This collection, which had belonged to a Roman nobleman,

Giampietro Campana, Marquese di Cavelli, was made up of twelve hundred Greek, Etruscan, and Roman pieces of jewelry. It went on display in the Louvre in 1863.

Cameos remained popular in the period, as did the neo-Renaissance style with enameled gold mounts. Following in the footsteps of his uncle, Napoleon I, Napoleon III encouraged the art of gemstone carving.

Floral motifs were highly fashionable. The plant repertoire expanded considerably and sparkled with diamonds. To make his jeweled branches lighter and more realistic, Oscar Massin perfected the "*tremblant*" (trembling) effect and reduced the settings. At the 1867 World's Fair, Empress Eugénie purchased a brooch in the shape of a lilac branch—one of the outstanding models of its kind—made by the jeweler Léon Rouvenat. The Boucheron jewelry house followed this example, producing brooches of the same type. Similarly naturalistic motifs included animals and insects, such as flies or butterflies, and then birds. The 1870s and 1880s saw the appearance of mythological creatures such as chimeras and dragons, which were later adopted by the art nouveau movement.

Finally, archeological discoveries in the valley of the Nile and the opening of the Suez Canal in 1869 revived the Egyptian style, as reflected in jewelry presented at the 1867 World's Fair featuring palm leaves, papyrus leaves, scarab beetles, and snakes.

Bracelet, Second Empire period • gold, cameo in coral, tortoiseshell

Necklace, c. 1900 •
platinum and gold, diamonds

The Belle Époque (1895–1914)

Context

Following the Franco-Prussian War in 1870 and the fall of the Second Empire, France went into a large-scale economic recession. A foreign clientele, notably American, partly compensated for the difficulties encountered by the French market, but the period was not favorable for jewelry, and no major changes took place. It wasn't until the mid-1890s that the Belle Époque style emerged, alongside art nouveau, and became the dominant fashion of the times. The expression "Belle Époque" was coined around 1919–20 in reference to those years of economic, social, and technological progress. The style is also known as the "garland" or Edwardian style, in reference to King Edward VII of

Great Britain, who reigned between 1901 and 1910. In a climate of prosperity and relative insouciance, the excellence of French jewelry making came to the fore.

Inspirations and Trends

The Belle Époque style was inspired by the French decorative arts of the eighteenth century, and was characterized by the use of platinum and the fine crafting of pieces. It emerged in the mid-nineteenth century when Empress Eugénie had numerous jewels remounted in the style of Louis XVI. Jewelers at the time were drawing inspiration from eighteenth-century ornamental designs. Louis Cartier embodied the garland style, creating wonderful combinations of floral, bow, and ribbon motifs. From 1910, the style was also developed by other houses, including Boucheron, Van Cleef & Arpels, and Chaumet.

The advent of platinum led to the replacement of silver in mounts, thereby making them airier and showing off the stones to better effect. These pieces required great skill, as platinum was difficult to work with. The metal was mostly used with two precious gems: pearls and diamonds. Diamonds were imported from South Africa following the discovery of deposits in 1867.

To meet the requirements of fashionable society at the time, these low-relief jewelry pieces were often transformable. In 1898, *L'Illustration* noted that "to satisfy the needs and desires of the woman who loves to wear her jewelry different ways, the pieces are generally put together in such a manner as to enable numerous transformations." A necklace, for example, might transform into a tiara.

World War I put an end to the Belle Époque style, and would have a significant influence on the art deco movement.

Brooch, c. 1900 •
platinum, sapphire, diamonds

Pendant-brooch by Henri Vever, c. 1900 • gold, enamel, opals, emeralds, diamonds

Art Nouveau (1895–1910)

Context

Art nouveau, also known as the "modern style," or "style Guimard" in France, lasted for only a short period of time, yet had a profound impact on jewelry history.

On December 26, 1895, Samuel Bing, a dealer in oriental objets d'art, opened the Maison de l'Art Nouveau, from which modern decorative art would borrow its name. Bing's gallery opening was welcomed with interest but also hostility. That same year, the Salon des Artistes Français accepted objets d'art for the first time. Henri Vever, one of the precursors of art nouveau, wrote in 1898, "It is indisputable that for several years . . . a considerable movement has been underway in the various branches of industrial art, and that attempts are being made from all sides to rejuvenate the old formulas used and abused by our predecessors." Art nouveau emerged out of a collective movement in reaction to the classicism of the time.

The 1900 World's Fair in Paris presented the work of a new generation of jewelers, including Vever, Lucien Gaillard, Georges Fouquet, and, in particular, René Lalique, the most innovative of them all. Without rejecting the contributions of previous eras, these jewelers developed a fresh interpretation of traditional themes and made use of new materials. French jewelry was booming and looking for new directions in which to expand.

Issue number 10 of the *Revue de la bijouterie, joaillerie, orfèvrerie* published in 1900 greeted the new fashion with enthusiasm: "So here, at the dawn of this century, is the French youth rid of its shackles, eager to give free rein to its ardent and impassioned imagination, our artists feeling an overwhelming desire to create and invent something new." The journal offered strong support for art nouveau over the dominant style of the time, Belle Époque.

Inspirations and Trends

Nature was one of the main sources of inspiration for art nouveau, especially flowers. Jewelers had inherited the tradition of floral-themed jewelry and were experimenting with a new, more modern approach that heightened the impression of movement and vitality. The appeal of Japanese art accentuated this trend. It was reflected in a book by Maurice Pillard Verneuil, *L'Animal dans la décoration*, published in 1898, which greatly influenced jewelry designers; it depicted butterflies, dragonflies, and fish that could be rendered in combinations of gemstones and enamel, birds with colorful plumage, bats and other nocturnal animals, reptiles, and even fantastical creatures.

The female figure was the second source of inspiration and at the heart of artistic creativity. Long hair was a pretext for a complex design. The American dancer Loïe Fuller was one of the muses of art nouveau. She invented new choreographies in which she danced with long swirling skirts illuminated with changing colors. The actress Sarah Bernhardt also personified art nouveau. She asked the painter Alphonse Mucha to design the posters for her plays, and she was the inspiration for Mucha's magnificent transformable snake bracelet, made for her by Fouquet. The latter would produce many pieces based on designs by the artist, and he commissioned Mucha to create the house's sumptuous boutique on Rue Royale.

The motif of the woman was also associated with flowers and animals. At the 1900 World's Fair, Paul and Henri Vever presented the Sylvia pendant: a butterfly-woman with a body carved in agate, combining gemstones with enamel.

Most art nouveau jewelry made only secondary use of the precious stones of the time—diamond, sapphire, emerald, and ruby—favoring decorative hardstones such as topaz, amethyst, agate, opal, ivory, and horn, among others; Lalique even used glass.

The movement was short-lived. The jewelry designs were initially very fashionable, before being copied on a wide scale. Immediately after 1900, many jewelers expanded their range to include art nouveau, with success. However, this new aesthetic began to receive criticism from 1902, and by 1904 artists were reacting negatively to it. Leading designers distanced themselves from art nouveau from around 1905. The style then began to go into decline, despite its commercial success. Large-scale production continued until 1914.

The sometimes excessive use of floral motifs or feminine curves that created flowing, entangled lines earned art nouveau the pejorative nickname "*style nouille*"—"noodle style." As Henri Vever put it, "The line is quite simply dead from exhaustion." World War I sounded the death knell for the movement.

Le Baiser ring by René Lalique, c. 1900–1905 • gold, pressed glass, enamel

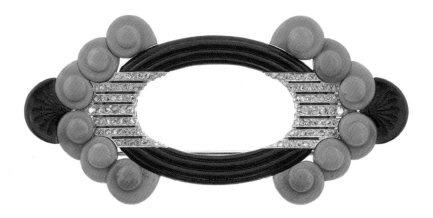

Brooch designed by René-Charles Massé for jeweler Louis Boucheron, presented at the Exposition Internationale des Arts Décoratifs et Industriels Modernes in Paris in 1925 • platinum and gold, coral, onyx, diamonds

Art Deco (1920–1935)

Context

After the end of World War I, French society underwent major transformations. A desire for renewal found expression in art deco. This "modern" style of the twentieth century spread worldwide in the interwar period, in all creative fields. It was an epoch that had a profound impact on jewelry history, with the emergence of inventive forms combined with extraordinarily delicate work in platinum.

Early signs of the art deco style appeared in 1905 with the birth of avant-garde movements, which were emerging all over Europe. Jewelers simplified the forms of their designs, heralding the geometric figures of art deco. This style spread rapidly after World War I. The sinuous lines of art nouveau, which had fallen victim to an affected academicism, were rejected. It was a revolution that responded to the demands of—and changes in—modern life. But this period of strong economic growth ended with the Wall Street Crash of 1929 and the Great Depression, whose repercussions were felt most strongly in France in the dark year of 1931.

The term art deco derives from the Exposition Internationale des Arts Décoratifs et Industriels Modernes that took place in Paris from April to October 1925.

Inspirations and Trends

Art deco jewelry broke completely with previous fashions and introduced an entirely new aesthetic. Countering the highly fluid and irrational style of art nouveau, characterized by its fauna- and flora-inspired motifs, artists chose sharper, more precise geometric forms to express the modernity of urban life. Geometry represented the quintessence of the modern world, and jewelry featured countless variations on the circle, triangle, rectangle, and square. Gem cutting also adopted geometric forms, including the round, trapeze, and baguette cuts. Among the prominent jewelry designers of the period were Gérard Sandoz and Georges and Jean Fouquet. In the 1930s, Van Cleef & Arpels invented its Serti Mystérieux setting, into which square-cut or calibrated gems were inserted without any visible prongs or metal.

This evolution in style took place in the context of various artistic developments, beginning with cubism, a movement that flourished between 1907 and 1914, led by the painters Georges Braque and Pablo Picasso. Post-cubist purism also influenced art deco. Le Corbusier and Amédée Ozenfant were its theorists, both advocating simple geometric forms. Futurism was another literary and artistic trend that developed from 1904 to 1920, celebrating speed and machines. The industrial world was a source of inspiration for the jewelry designers Jean Després and Raymond Templier.

In 1909, Serge Diaghilev's famous Ballets Russes began an international tour, starting in Paris. On Diaghilev's initiative, these ballets incorporated all forms of artistic expression, inspiring artists with their colorful aesthetic—colors that were reflected in the choice of stones set in platinum, such as amethyst, topaz, onyx, turquoise, coral, and lapis lazuli.

Closely linked with the emergence of cubism, African art became highly popular, notably its use of the broken

Ring, c. 1930 •
platinum, diamonds

line and spiral motifs. In 1925, Josephine Baker's *Revue nègre* show was a huge success in France. Among the jewelry designs presented at the 1931 Exposition Coloniale (Colonial Exhibition) were brooches and pendants with African mask motifs.

Ancient Egypt also came back into fashion, thanks to Howard Carter's discovery of the tomb of Tutankhamun in 1922. As in the late eighteenth and mid-nineteenth centuries, Egyptian motifs were all the rage, but this time the phenomenon was amplified by the media and film industry. Jewelry featured scarab beetles, pyramids, and sphinxes.

The use of mythological figures reflected an enduring taste for antiquity. Greek culture, which had been popular in the late eighteenth century, held new appeal. Jewelers also drew inspiration from the Far East, particularly China and Japan, borrowing iconographic elements such as masks, pagodas, and landscapes, and using materials such as jade.

Art deco designs favored flora over fauna, with a penchant for compositions of stylized flowers. The rose, as found in eighteenth-century porcelain, was selected and stylized in 1908–1909 by the illustrator and designer Paul Iribe to decorate dresses by the couturier Paul Poiret. Inspired by the flower, Poiret made it his hallmark: he named one of his daughters Rosine and founded a perfume laboratory named Les Parfums de Rosine. Thanks to the renown of "*la rose d'Iribe*," this motif was widely adopted in the world of haute couture and jewelry (Van Cleef & Arpels, Lacloche, Mauboussin).

Sautoir by Van Cleef & Arpels, 1928 • platinum, diamonds

Jeep de la Libération brooch
by Mauboussin, c. 1945 • gold
and platinum, diamonds, rubies,
sapphires

The 1940s

Context

The 1937 World's Fair held in Paris, officially titled Exposition International des Arts et Techniques Appliqués à la Vie Moderne, prefigured a new style that would develop in the 1940s, moving away from art deco. It opened in a particularly tense international context. The Spanish Civil War was raging. At the fair, the grandiose pavilions of Hitlerian Germany and Stalinist Russia faced each other in confrontation. Two years later, war broke out. While jewelry continued to be produced and sold, it was only accessible to certain people and in certain regions. The conflict led to the rationing of precious metals in France and the interruption of gem imports from the East, while many jewelers were called up for military service. Those jewelers who remained in business had to adapt to the situation in imaginative ways. An article

in *L'Officiel de la couture et de la mode de Paris* of May 1940 commented, "As an eminently luxurious business, French jewelry could not hope to survive these hard times without changing the look and purpose of its products."

As a result of the war, jewelry became a safe investment for some, losing its ornamental role. In 1942, Georges Fouquet wrote in the book *L'Orfèvrerie, la joaillerie*, "Buyers, many of whom are newcomers as jewelry collectors, are focusing their attention more on valuable gems. Jewelry is losing its artistic and decorative value and is becoming an investment, a form of capital, that has the added advantage of being easily transportable." The jewelry industry may have adapted, but it emerged exhausted from those dark days.

Influences and Trends

Over the course of the decade, geometric forms softened, and curving lines made a comeback for larger jewelry pieces. The break with art deco was also characterized by the return of yellow or rose gold, the near absence of gems, and the use of synthetic stones. Yellow gold was often worked to resemble a fabric, with draping or pleats, or lace with bow motifs. Its voluminous forms usually made up for the scarcity of gems. Gold was also fashioned into snake, spring, or "tubogas" chains (the latter imitating a flexible metal gas tube).

Jewelry inspiration was primarily naturalistic. Brooches often featured floral bouquets in gold with sapphires, rubies, and diamonds. In reference to this trend, the General Report of the 1937 Exposition Internationale des Arts et des Techniques Appliqués à la Vie Moderne noted that "the Admission Committee was seeing designs that betrayed an excessive tendency to use a barely transposed floral decoration." The fashion was also on display at the 1941 Foire de Lyon, notably in Boucheron's Bouquet de Violettes brooch. Designers were once more exploring animal themes, largely ignored during the art deco period. Their pieces showed off shimmering colors, often in bird or butterfly motifs.

Patriotic themes also made an appearance in this decade. In 1942, in its Paris store, Cartier presented a brooch with a bird in a cage in the colors of the French flag—a piece designed by Jeanne Toussaint, the house's director of high jewelry, and Peter Lemarchand. Symbolizing the French people under the Occupation, the piece represented Cartier's support for the Resistance movement. Some of General de Gaulle's speeches were written at Jacques Cartier's office in London. Two years later, in 1944, a tricolor brooch depicting a bird at the open door of a cage would this time represent the Liberation. In similar spirit, Mauboussin celebrated the arrival of the American forces with the Jeep de la Libération brooch, studded with diamonds, rubies, and sapphires. Van Cleef & Arpels, in turn, created the Pax clip and Le Flambeau de la Libération.

After the war, many jewelry items that were considered outdated were unmounted. Scornfully nicknamed "BOF"—*beurre, œufs, fromage* (butter, eggs, cheese)—as the nouveaux riches who had made their money on the black market were called, the jewelry of the 1940s was, to quote Jean Mauboussin, "the jewelry of a time of crisis, so it made sense that it should disappear when that time came to an end."

Bracelet and earrings by Boucheron, c. 1940 • gold and platinum, graduated rubies, diamonds

Necklace and ear clips,
c. 1950 • gold and platinum,
diamonds

The 1950s

Context

After years of wartime and hardship, France entered a period of growth that brought about profound economic and social changes, stimulating every creative field. Christian Dior made his mark on the epoch with his invention of the New Look, which presented a more modern image of women. Where jewelry was concerned, France still set the tone, but Italy began to establish a more eclectic, whimsical style. This taste for whimsy was also developing in the United States, following its success in France in the 1930s.

Influences and Trends

Several trends emerged from this decade bridging the postwar period and the economic boom of the 1960s. Jewelry was smaller but of higher quality. Mounts were highly ingenious in design. Settings generally had no visible prongs.

Naturalism was very present, with leaves and feathers being dominant themes. Naturalistic animal motifs were also popular. Designs featured birds, ladybugs, and tortoises, and domestic animals such as rabbits, cats, and dogs (mostly basset hounds and poodles) could be spotted in most jewelers' shop windows.

The 1950s also saw the return of platinum and white gold, yellow gold having been favored in the previous decade. Rubies, sapphires, emeralds, and especially diamonds reappeared and were given pride of place in pieces that evoked movement and cascades. Stunning combinations of gemstones, such as rubies with turquoises, were produced toward the end of this period.

While these themes may appear to have been directly inherited from the 1940s, the gold was worked in a more complex manner, notably using all sorts of wire. Smooth, twisted, or braided, the wirework was still suggestive of fabric and trimmings, but was lighter and more flexible.

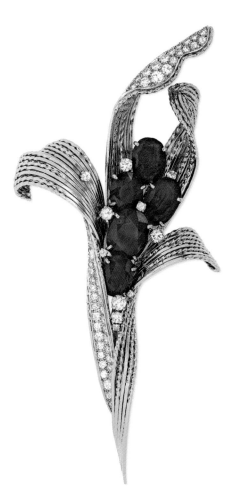

Brooch by Sterlé, 1955 •
gold, rubies, diamonds

Materials

Plate 3 from *Le Bijou: Revue artistique et industrielle*
le la bijouterie, joaillerie, orfèvrerie, musée pratique
à l'usage des joailliers, bijoutiers, orfèvres, estampeurs,
graveurs, peintres, J. Rothschild (ed.), 1900

Precious Metals

T hree precious metals are used in antique jewelry: gold, platinum, and silver. These metals form the basic structure of jewelry pieces.

Gold

Of all the precious metals, gold has always been the most coveted throughout history. Humans have consistently been drawn to its inherent beauty, great malleability, and resistance to corrosion. It is traditionally the most frequently used metal of the three.

Characteristics

The chemical symbol for this yellow-colored metal, Au, comes from the Latin *aurum* (as does the French word for gold, *or*). Pure gold is unaffected by air and water, which is doubtless why it is so highly prized. It is the most malleable and ductile of all metals. It can be melted without losing strength, and pressed into a leaf with a thickness of 1/10,000 mm. It also has a high density, almost twice that of lead.

Deposits

Gold is found in its natural state in the form of primary and secondary deposits. Primary deposits are the solid gold-bearing rocks or metallic seams, while secondary deposits refer to the metal-bearing alluviums derived from the erosion of gold-bearing rocks and their deposits in rivers in the form of sediment. Gold is present in most countries, but the main production sites have varied throughout the ages; they notably include South Africa, the United States, Australia, and Russia.

"Tank" bracelets,
c. 1940 • gold

History

Gold mining has been recorded since the fifth century BCE in Varna, Bulgaria. In ancient Egypt, the finely chased parures of the pharaohs are wonderful examples of Egyptian craftsmen's skills. The ancient Greeks and Romans produced gold for purposes of adornment and as a currency. The increasing demand for jewelry was such that Pliny wrote, "The worst crime in the history of mankind was committed by the man who first put gold on his fingers." On the other side of the world, the Incas and Aztecs used gold to honor their gods.

The precious metal was one of the reasons for the conquest of the New World. When Christopher Columbus reached the Bahamas on October 12, 1492, the goal was to appropriate the riches of the Indies and the Far East. In the mid-nineteenth century, the discovery of a gold nugget in California by James W. Marshall launched the gold rush. This phenomenon marked the beginning of the contemporary history of gold. While it continues to symbolize wealth and power, this precious metal is now far more accessible.

Fineness and colors

The "fineness" indicates the purity of gold by expressing the proportion of the mass of pure metal relative to the total mass of the alloy containing it. As gold is extremely malleable, it is often alloyed with other metals such as silver, copper, or zinc in order to increase its strength. The proportion of pure gold in an alloy is expressed in millesimals or parts per thousand (‰). In France, the millesimal has replaced the karat (k) since 1995. Pure gold corresponds to 1,000 fineness (or 24k). Gold with a millesimal fineness of 750 (18k) was required for jewelry production in France up until 1994.

The composition of the alloy also gives gold its color. Yellow gold is usually an alloy of gold (750 ‰), silver (approximately 180 ‰), and copper (approximately 70 ‰). Rose (or pink) gold is made up of gold (750 ‰), copper (approximately 200 ‰), and silver (approximately 50 ‰). Finally, gray gold is generally made up of gold (750 ‰), palladium (approximately 150 ‰), and silver (approximately 100 ‰).

Hallmarks

Works of precious metal commercialized in France must be done so in accordance with their fineness. The first attempts at the regulation of gold date from Roman times. Then, in 1260, Étienne Boileau, Prévôt de Paris under Louis IX, drew up *Le Livre des métiers* (the Book of Trades), which regulated the trade guilds. The *Charte parisienne des Orfèvres* (Parisian Charter of Goldsmiths) set out various requirements guaranteeing the fineness of works in gold. Regulations have continued to evolve since then. A law on the control of fineness and the collection of fees for assay of gold and silver materials was enacted on 19 Brumaire, year VI (November 9, 1797). Commonly known as the Loi de Brumaire, it replaced the rules of the ancien régime. It was later amended to accommodate evolving techniques.

Master's or maker's mark

The diamond shape of this mark was laid down by the decree of the Administration des Monnaies of 17 Nivôse, year VI (January 6, 1798). Article 9 reads, "The maker's mark is the initial letter of his name, with a symbol." In practice, it is usually two initials: that of the first name followed by that of the family name. The maker must register with the *bureau de garantie* (assay office), in other words, with the customs authorities.

Assay office mark

The assay mark attests that the proportion of gold in the work complies with applicable laws. The Loi de Brumaire (Art. 4) established three grades of millesimal fineness for gold: 920, 840, and 750. Two extra grades were added in 1994: 585 and 375.

Symbols

In the late eighteenth and early nineteenth centuries, the hallmark was symbolized by a rooster in France. From 1838 to the present, the assay office mark for Paris has been an eagle head; for the provinces, it was a horse's head from 1838 to 1919, replaced in 1919 by an eagle head. Secondhand and imported works are also subject to laws. The first import mark for gold and silver appeared in 1838, and was modified in 1864. The owl hallmark symbolizing an uncertain or foreign origin is often found on antique jewelry. The hallmark is located on the band (shank) of a ring and on the clasp of a necklace, bracelet, or back of an earring. However, the hallmarks on antique jewelry are often worn and require careful examination.

Determination of purity

In the absence of a hallmark, gold can be tested for purity with an assaying tool (a touchstone) or, nowadays, in a laboratory using spectrometry. The former technique is very simple: the metal is rubbed on the touchstone to leave a visible trace. Other traces are left on the same touchstone with an alloy of known purity (the control). Each is then uniformly dampened with a previously measured and prepared acid solution called aqua regia ("royal water"): various proportions of hydrochloric acid and of nitric acid that are used for each gold grade (over 18k, between 14k and 18k, and below 14k). The richer the alloy in gold, the more brilliant and yellow the streaks left on the stone. Today, X-ray fluorescence spectrometry rapidly determines the precise chemical composition of gold alloys in a non-destructive manner.

Care

Gold can be simply cleaned with a soft brush and soapy water. Yellow gold can tarnish. If white gold becomes grayish, it needs to be repolished or rhodium-plated to renew its shine.

Main French hallmarks for gold

From 1798 to 1809

Paris: rooster head · Departments: rooster head

From 1809 to 1819

Paris: rooster head · Departments: rooster head

From 1819 to 1838

Paris: ram head · Departments: 9 divisional hallmarks

From 1838 to 1919

Paris: eagle head, from 1838 to 1847, slight variation · Departments: horse head

From 1919 to the present

Eagle head

Secondhand works of foreign or uncertain origin: owl · Low-fineness works: ET

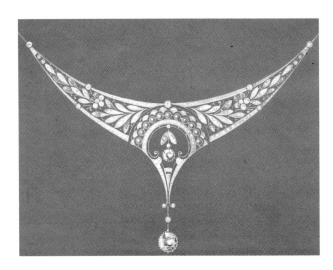

Sketch for a necklace, c. 1900 •
platinum, diamonds

Platinum

This rare, gray-white metal is prized for certain properties that make it unique. It has been used in jewelry since the nineteenth century.

Characteristics

Its name comes from the Spanish *platina*, meaning "little silver," and it has the chemical symbol Pt. Platinum is one of the densest metals: it has a density of 21.5 grams per cubic centimeter, which is higher than that of silver (10.5 grams) and gold (19.3 grams). Platinum is extremely resistant to heat, making it a challenging metal to work with: its melting point is 3,221°F (1,772°C). It is resistant to almost all acids. It is highly malleable, as well as soft and elastic.

Deposits

Platinum is thirty times rarer than gold. It is extracted from alluvial sands and usually takes the form of small, rounded steel-gray nuggets or grains. Until 1825, it came solely from South America. Today, platinum reserves are mainly in South Africa and Russia.

History

Platinum is considered a recent metal, yet its history can be traced all the way back to the Eighteenth Dynasty of Egypt (1550–1292 BCE), as it has been found in a few items of jewelry belonging to the pharaohs of this period. During antiquity, it was worked very little. However, it was used by the pre-Columbian Native Americans. Its discovery by Europeans is attributed to a Spanish officer, Don Antonio de Ulloa, in 1735, who recorded platinum for the first time in his book *Relación histórica del viaje a la America meridional* (Historical Account of the Trip to South America). The strange properties of the metal surprised European scientists. In 1751, Swedish scientist Henrik Teofilus Scheffer designated it a metal in its own right. In 1780, Louis XVI declared that it was the only metal worthy of kings; the goldsmith Marc-Étienne Janety made several pieces in platinum for him. In 1789, the French chemist Pierre-François Chabaneau was the first to produce malleable platinum.

In the nineteenth century, the use of this metal became more widespread, and platinum jewelry was presented at the Exposition Publique des Produits de l'Industrie Française (Public Exhibition of Products of French Industry) in 1802. Louis-François Cartier increased its use during the second half of the nineteenth century. Thanks to this development, jewelry makers gradually abandoned the use of double-metal stone settings (silver in the upper part and gold in the lower part).

Platinum was considered a precious metal in many fields. It was used for military purposes in World War I, and in the United Kingdom it was even forbidden to sell it to private individuals. From the early twentieth century until World War II, platinum was in its prime. Its success reached Hollywood, where, in 1931, Frank Capra made *Platinum Blonde*—the movie that launched the legendary "platinum blonde," as embodied by Jean Harlow. During World War II, platinum was once again commandeered by the military industry. At the end of the war, it made a comeback in jewelry, with geometric forms reminiscent of the art deco style.

Fineness

Platinum used in jewelry making is very pure. Its fineness is measured in millesimals (‰). It is alloyed with other metals that harden it, particularly iridium, palladium, and copper.

Hallmarks

The French decree of December 5, 1912, introduced hallmarks for works made wholly or partly of platinum. The assay office mark is a dog head. A mascaron is stamped on secondhand platinum works of French or foreign origin.

Determination of purity

Like gold or silver, the fineness of platinum is determined using a touchstone or by spectrometry.

Care

Platinum can be cleaned with soapy water. Although platinum is a durable metal, it can be damaged if knocked.

Main French hallmarks for platinum

From 1912 to the present

Dog head

Secondhand works of foreign or uncertain origin

Mascaron

Ring by Jean Després,
c. 1930 • silver

Silver

Silver is a metal with a light to very light neutral gray color.
It is the most common precious metal in the world.

Characteristics

The chemical symbol of silver, Ag, comes
from the Latin *argentum* (as does the
French *argent*), derived from the Greek
argos, meaning "shining, white" and also
the Sanskrit *arjuna*, meaning "bright,
white." Silver's good malleability lends
itself to jewelry making. However, sulfur in
the air causes silver to oxidize (tarnish).

Deposits

Silver is rare in its natural state and is most
often found combined with other metals. It
is extracted from silver-rich mines or from
gold, lead, copper, or zinc mines. Found all
over the globe, it is a hundred times more
abundant than gold. The principal silver-
producing countries are Mexico, Peru,
Russia, and the United States.

History

Humans have made jewelry from silver
since the earliest times. Every era and
every country has added its contribution.
After gold and copper, silver is one of
the first metals that people learned to
extract. It first appeared in Asia Minor
and in the Near East, in the second
half of the fourth millennium BCE. In
ancient Egypt, it was more precious than
gold until the third millennium BCE. In
the first century CE, Pliny described it
as the "next folly of mankind." Silver
production increased considerably in
Europe between the thirteenth and
fifteenth centuries. The metal is also
closely linked to the history of alchemy.
In the cupellation process, lead appears
to transform into silver—an experiment

that may have inspired the alchemists' theories of transmutation.

During the Spanish conquest of the Americas, deposits were discovered in Mexico, then in Peru, whereas mines in Europe were becoming exhausted. In the nineteenth century, silver was used in jewelry making for setting diamonds, before being replaced by platinum, then gray gold.

Fineness

Silver is a soft metal that cannot be used pure. Copper is therefore often used as an alloy element, as is gold at times.

The fineness of silver is expressed in millesimals (‰). There are two main silver standards of millesimal fineness: The French 1st standard, like Sterling silver, is made up of silver (925 ‰) and copper (75 ‰). The French 2nd standard is silver (800 ‰) and copper (200 ‰). When "solid" silver (over 800 ‰) is covered in gold, it is called silver-gilt or vermeil.

Hallmarks

Assay marks for silver jewelry were the head of Liberty in the late eighteenth century, and the fasces and hare head in the early nineteenth century. Numerous animal figures (butterfly, ray, snail) followed for the provincial marks. From 1838, a wild boar head was used for Paris and a crab for the provinces. The boar head was abandoned in 1962 and was replaced by the crab for the whole of France until 1984.

Determination of purity

In the absence of a millesimal number, silver fineness can be determined using a touchstone and by spectrometry. There is also a wet assay method specific to silver, which was discovered by Joseph Louis Gay-Lussac and adopted in 1830: the weight of the standard salt solution required for the precipitation of silver

to occur is compared before and after the assay.

Care

Silver is prone to scratches and blackening. Besides the various cleaning products available in stores, bicarbonate of soda can be used.

Main French hallmarks for silver

From 1798 to 1809

Fasces

From 1809 to 1819

Paris: fasces with axe to the left

Departments: fasces with axe to the right

From 1819 to 1838

Paris: hare head

Departments: 9 divisional hallmarks

From 1838 to the present

Paris: wild boar head

Departments: crab

Secondhand works of foreign or uncertain origin: swan

Low-fineness works: ET

Non-Precious Materials

Base metals and other non-precious materials are frequently used in jewelry making, especially for "imitation" or "costume" jewelry, which appeared in the early eighteenth century and became increasingly popular through the nineteenth century. These pieces copied fine jewelry designs but were made with non-precious materials. In 1873, the Chambre Syndicale de la Bijouterie de Fantaisie (Costume Jewelry Trade Association) was founded. The mechanization of manufacturing processes enabled jewelry production to keep up with the fashions of the day. In the early twentieth century, the development of these production methods was embraced by prestigious couture houses, including Chanel.

Base Metals

Unlike precious metals, base metals have a lower chemical resistance. Copper, iron, and aluminum are among those most frequently used in antique jewelry.

Copper

Copper is a ductile and malleable metal with a reddish-brown color. It was one of the first metals to be used by humans. Items of jewelry dating from the eighth and seventh millennia BCE have been discovered in Iran.

Tiara, early nineteenth
century • iron

Iron

Iron was used to make jewelry in the
eighteenth and nineteenth centuries. After
Napoleon's conquest of Prussia in 1806,
the Royal Berlin Foundry, established
in 1804, fell into the hands of the French,
and the French Empire used the German
molds to produce necklaces and bracelets.
Out of patriotism and a need to raise
funds in the war against Napoleon, the
German people traded their jewelry made
of precious materials for jewelry in iron.
These pieces often bore the inscription
"I gave gold in exchange for iron." After
the war, the fashion spread throughout
Europe in the 1820s. Iron was also used
to produce the historical-style jewelry
that was popular in the nineteenth
century. It can be seen in mourning
jewelry, due to its black color and the
prevailing tradition that forbade the
wearing of gold during mourning.

Aluminum

Aluminum is a light, white, and highly
malleable metal. It was developed in France
from 1854 thanks to the chemist Henri
Sainte-Claire Deville. Rare examples of
jewelry in aluminum with a gold mount
include a bracelet presented to Queen
Victoria by Napoleon III at the 1855 World's
Fair in Paris. The price of these early
aluminum pieces was even higher than that
of jewelry made of precious metals.

During World War I, soldiers would
craft jewelry mostly out of aluminum, such
as "trench rings" made from shell fuzes.
Nickel from German bullets was also a
highly sought-after material.

Base Metal Alloys

Brass

Brass is a yellow-colored alloy mostly composed of copper and zinc. Mentioned in records dating back to 500 CE, it is often used in jewelry to imitate gold.

Nickel silver

Nickel silver is an alloy principally composed of copper, zinc, and nickel. It is white in color and resembles silver. It was discovered between 1819 and 1823 by the Lyon-based engineers Maillet and Chorier, for whom the French word for this metal, *maillechort*, was named.

Pomponne

Pomponne is a copper-based alloy used to imitate gold. It was developed in the late eighteenth century by two goldsmiths, Turgot and Daumy, who were based at the Pomponne mansion on Rue de la Verrerie in Paris. This alloy was used by jewelry makers until the late nineteenth century, when it was replaced by gold plate.

Gold Plate and Silver Plate

Precious metals have long been used to coat base metals. Gold and silver plate consists of a base metal or a base metal alloy, whose surface is covered or plated with a thin layer of the precious metal. This technique was developed over the course of the nineteenth century. Today, French legislation requires a minimum thickness of 3 microns of gold for gold plate; below this threshold, the relevant term is *doré*, meaning gilded. For silver plate, a minimum thickness of 10 microns of silver is required by French law.

Care

The thin plating on a piece of jewelry deteriorates on contact with the skin and tarnishes. To keep gold- and silver-plated jewelry in good condition, it must be cleaned regularly. Soapy water is usually sufficient.

Plate 41 from *Fantaisies décoratives* by Jules Habert-Dys, 1887

Natural Materials

Hair

The exchanging or gifting of a lock of hair appears to date back to the fourteenth century. Whether a token of love or a souvenir of someone lost or far away, this tiny but enduring fragment of a loved one was often enclosed in a piece of jewelry in the eighteenth century. Placed under glass, the hair was braided, finely cut, or reduced to dust. It sometimes formed lovers' crowned initials or a sentimental landscape. The *Manuel du voyageur à Paris* (Travelers Guide to Paris) from 1800 includes the following recommendation: "Visitors, if you have left behind in your home country someone whom you miss and to whom you wish to send a monument of your remembrance and a small portion of yourself, cut a few locks of your hair and take them to no. 86 Rue Denis; a skilled artisan will compose with them a symbol or allegorical subject as true to life as a painting! Have a ring or locket enhanced in this manner; these little things keep the affection alive and are conducive to faithfulness."

Before and during the Revolution, many such pieces were produced. The Musée Carnavalet in Paris holds a veritable relic in the form of a pendant containing the hair of Marie Antoinette. By 1840, jewelry pieces composed of hair were becoming considerably larger in size. Using bobbins on a loom, entire bracelets were made of braided and twisted hair, and the clasp could be a miniature portrait of someone held dear. These pieces were crafted by jewelers specialized in the technique, and it was very important that the person's actual hair was used, not a substitute.

From the mid-nineteenth century onward, the use of hair was gradually replaced by photographs. However, numerous lockets contained both mementos of a loved one: a lock of hair and a photographic portrait. These intimate pieces of jewelry capture the presence of the absent person, maintaining a bond that extends beyond death. Queen Victoria favored this fashion after the death of her beloved Prince Albert in 1861. The use of hair in sentimental jewelry was progressively abandoned after 1920.

Bracelet, c. 1820 • gold, enamel, braided or interwoven locks of hair

"Esclavage" (slavery) necklace, early nineteenth century • gold, enamel

Wood

Easy to work with, wood can be used to create a variety of forms in different shades of color. In the nineteenth century, it was used for combs, which were a very popular hair ornament at the time, owing to the fashion for chignons. The material then fell out of fashion, before making a return after World War I. In 1919, Van Cleef & Arpels launched a line called Touch Wood, targeting a less affluent clientele. But it wasn't until the 1970s that the luxury houses on Place Vendôme adopted this material again.

Enamel

Enamel is made from a powdered substance (glass) that produces a vitreous material on melting. Its color is obtained from metal oxides: cobalt for blue, tin for white, manganese for black, and so on. The powdered glass is applied cold to a metal surface, then the whole piece is fired to fuse it permanently to its base. Gold, copper, iron, and silver can all be enameled. The enameling process, for which several techniques exist, can be traced back to antiquity, and was highly fashionable in the nineteenth and early twentieth centuries. In champlevé enamel, recesses, or cells, are dug out of the metal to match the intended design. In cloisonné enamel, thin wires are soldered to the metal surface to create compartments, or cells, into which the enamel is placed. Unlike the previous techniques, in plique-à-jour enamel there is no metal backing in its final state, creating a stained-glass effect. This medieval technique was revived in the late nineteenth century. From the 1890s, it was used by artists and designers of the art nouveau movement.

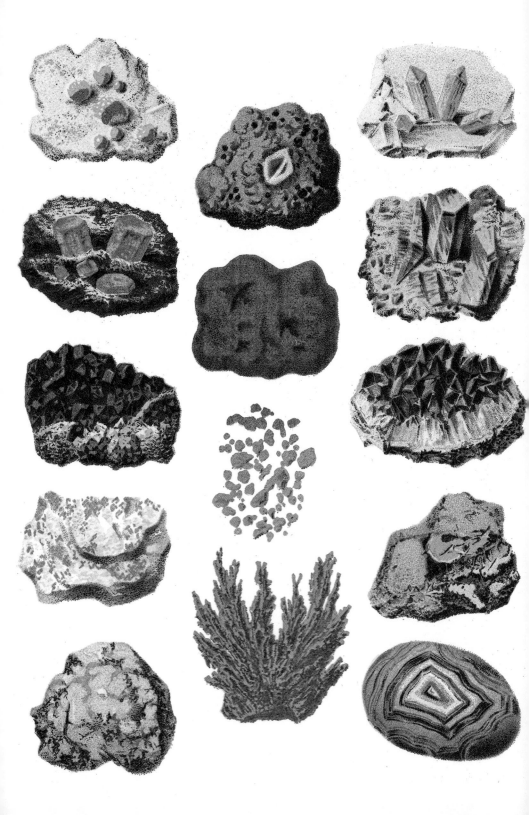

Gemstones

Plate from *Les Pierres précieuses et les principaux ornements*
by Jean Rambosson, 1870

Among the several thousand minerals that exist, only about fifty gemstones are commonly used in jewelry. Of these, twenty-one are characteristic of antique jewelry and are described in this chapter. In France, the law of August 1, 1905, distinguishes "precious stones" (diamonds, rubies, sapphires, and emeralds) from other "semiprecious" stones used in jewelry: "hardstones" and "ornamental stones." Today, since the French decree no. 2002-65 of January 14, 2002, all of these gems are grouped under the name "gemstones." The terms of the decree also apply to organic materials of plant or animal origin traditionally used in jewelry, as well as pearls.

Since antiquity, the unit of mass most commonly used in international commerce has been the carat. This word most likely derives from the use of the carob bean as a unit of weight. The metric carat (abbreviation: ct or mct) was introduced in 1907; prior to this date, the unit varied from country to country. The metric carat is equal to 0.20 grams. The carat, a unit of mass, should not be confused with the karat (k), a unit measuring the purity of gold.

Agate

Characteristics
Agate is a variety of chalcedony (microcrystalline silica). Its name may derive from the Acate River (or Dirillo) in Sicily, where the stone was found in abundance.

History
This gemstone has been prized since antiquity. It comes in many different forms. One particular type is highly sought after for making cameos; when the stone is made up of different colored bands, it can be carved in relief to obtain a motif.

Color(s)
Agate exists in numerous colors, with the dominant shades being gray, whitish-gray, white, and brown. It can also contain various minerals that form patterns evocative of plants or landscapes.

Provenance
Until 1830, the largest deposits were located in the region of Idar-Oberstein in Germany. Seams discovered in Brazil in 1827 constitute the main sources of supply today. Agate is also found in Australia and China.

Aquamarine

Characteristics

Aquamarine is a variety of beryl, as is emerald. Its name comes from the Latin *aqua marina*, meaning "seawater." One legend describes aquamarine as the treasure of nymphs. Sailors used it as a lucky charm, believing it to have the power to calm the waves.

History

Aquamarine was particularly appreciated by art deco designers; it was often featured in the center of their geometric compositions. It was also popular in the 1950s.

Color(s)

Ranging from light to bright blue to slightly greenish, its color is due to traces of iron in beryl's crystal structure.

Provenance

Brazilian aquamarines were discovered by the governor Duarte de Costa between 1551 and 1554. The most renowned specimens from Brazil were those of Santa Maria de Itabira, found in the early twentieth century. The main producers are now Brazil, Madagascar, Pakistan, and Afghanistan.

Medallion-brooch, Second Empire period • gold, enamel, carved agate cameo

Amethyst

Characteristics

Amethyst is a variety of quartz (monocrystalline silica). Its name comes from an ancient Greek word, which, literally translated, means "not intoxicated"; because its color is similar to that of wine, it was believed, in antiquity, to prevent drunkenness.

History

Mentioned in the Bible, amethyst was used by the ancient Egyptians. In the Middle Ages, it adorned the rings worn by bishops. Under the Restoration in France (1814–1830), renewed trade relations with Brazil contributed to its commercialization around the world.

Color(s)

The color of amethyst, which ranges from deep mauve to pale violet, is due to traces of iron.

Provenance

Amethyst is relatively abundant around the world. The largest deposits are in Brazil, Uruguay, Bolivia, and Madagascar.

Necklace, c. 1830 •
gold, amethysts

Ring by Sterlé, c. 1955 •
gold and platinum,
citrine, diamonds

Citrine

Characteristics

Citrine belongs to the quartz family
(monocrystalline silica). Its name comes
from the Latin *citrus*, meaning "lemon,"
owing to its yellow color. Natural citrines
are rare; they are most often heat-treated
amethysts.

History

Citrine was one of the most commonly
used stones during the reign of Charles X
and the July Monarchy (1830–1848).

Color(s)

Its color is derived from the presence of
aluminum and iron, and ranges from pale
to dark yellow to a "madeira" brownish-
orange.

Provenance

Citrine deposits are generally found in the
same locations as amethyst.

Coral

Characteristics
Coral is the calcareous exoskeleton secreted by colonies of tiny marine animals called polyps. In the eighteenth century, the naturalist Jean-André Peyssonnel identified corals as belonging to the animal kingdom.

History
Coral has been known and used since antiquity, but it was in great favor in the nineteenth century during the two French Empires, notably for use in jewelry parures and hair combs. Art nouveau jewelers also appreciated coral. In 1901, the *Revue de la bijouterie, joaillerie, orfèvrerie* wrote, "The divers of the Mediterranean are happy; there's no doubt that coral is back in fashion." In art deco pieces, coral was combined with onyx, turquoise, or lapis lazuli.

Color(s)
Due to the presence of natural organic pigments related to carotene, the colors of coral range from white to blood red. The latter is the most sought after in jewelry making. Keratinous black coral has been much less in demand, except in the 1920s.

Provenance
Coral requires calm, clear, and temperate waters at 55°F–60°F (13°C–16°C). Coral fishing has existed since antiquity in the Mediterranean. In France, it developed in the eighteenth century with the Compagnie Royale d'Afrique (Royal African Company). After the Revolution, the Italian coral fishing industry took over, mainly at Torre del Greco in Naples. In the mid-nineteenth century, several hundred coral workers were still operating in France, between Marseille and Cassis. After World War I, coral mostly came from Japan. Coral is also found in the seas between Japan and the Malay Archipelago, and in the Indian Ocean. Previously fished by free divers, coral has been harvested by dragging nets since the nineteenth century.

France, along with more than 180 other countries, is a member of the Washington Convention of March 3, 1973, known as the CITES: Convention on International Trade in Endangered Species of Wild Fauna and Flora. Today, numerous coral species are protected by the CITES.

Dress clip by Boucheron, c. 1950 • platinum and gold, enamel, coral, diamonds

Bracelet, c. 1805–1815 •
gold, carved carnelian cameo

Carnelian

Characteristics

Carnelian is a variety of chalcedony (microcrystalline silica). Its name, often associated with the red-colored fruit of the Cornelian cherry or European cornel, in fact derives from the ancient Sardinian port of Cornus.

History

Carnelian has been prized since antiquity. It was used in the nineteenth century to make intaglio carvings.

Color(s)

Its color is due to the presence of iron and ranges from orange to red, with a translucent to opaque appearance.

Provenance

Carnelian is mostly found in Brazil, Uruguay, and India.

Necklace by Jean Fouquet,
c. 1928 • enamel, rock crystal,
aquamarine, diamonds

Rock Crystal

Characteristics

Rock crystal is a variety of quartz
(monocrystalline silica). The word "crystal"
derives from the Greek *krystallos*, meaning
"ice." In ancient times, this stone was
thought to be eternal ice. Alternative names
include quartz crystal or quartz rock.

History

Its use can be traced back to the Mesolithic
period (between 8000 and 5000 BCE).
It was fashionable in the art deco era, in
combination with diamonds.

Color(s)

Rock crystal is colorless.

Provenance

Rock crystal deposits are widespread
throughout the world. The main producing
countries are Brazil, India, Switzerland,
and the United States. In France, one of
the most famous deposits—La Gardette
in Villard-Notre-Dame, in the Alps—
was discovered in the early eighteenth
century and is reputed for its magnificent
transparent crystals.

Diamond

Characteristics

Diamond is the hardest natural material known to date. The ancient Greeks called it *adamas*, meaning "invincible" or "indestructible." It is composed of pure carbon that has crystallized at depths of over 95 miles (150 km) in the mantle below the earth's crust, as a result of high pressures and temperatures. Very old and deep eruptions, known as kimberlitic eruptions, caused the diamonds to rise to the surface, where they are currently extracted. There are no more eruptions of this type on Earth, and the available diamond resources are therefore finite.

History

India is the oldest diamond-producing country, where the stone has been mined since at least 800 BCE. The exportation and trade of diamonds began around 400 BCE. From antiquity to the eighteenth century, all diamonds came from India. In 1725, the discovery of deposits in Brazil (Diamantina) led to a diamond rush from 1727 to 1771. These diamonds poured into Europe for a century, but extensive mining of the site brought about a fall in supply in the mid-nineteenth century. Prices tripled from 1830 to 1869, and although demand for diamonds remained present, other less costly gemstones were preferred.

In 1866, in South Africa, the young Erasmus Jacobs brought his sister some pretty stones from the Orange River to play with. One of them had a bright sparkle to it and was noticed by a neighbor, who offered to buy the stone; the family gave it to him. It turned out to be a 21.24-carat diamond—the first ever diamond found in South Africa—and was named the Eureka Diamond. In May 1871, a rumor spread that diamonds had been discovered at the De Beer farm, sparking a diamond hunt. In the late nineteenth century, South African deposits brought considerable quantities of diamonds onto the market. In 1880, the De Beers Mining Company Ltd. was founded. Long the sole owner of all of the world's diamond mines (mostly in South Africa), De Beers purchased the diamonds mined by other companies as each new deposit was discovered (in Angola, Sierra Leone, Congo, then in Russia from the 1950s). Today, the company that enjoyed a near-monopoly until the 2000s shares the market, notably with the Alrosa (Russia), Dominion (Canadian), and Rio Tinto (Anglo-Australian) groups.

Color(s)

Diamond is usually colorless, but chemical elements can color the gem. There are yellow, blue, red, green, and pink diamonds, among others.

Provenance

The first large diamond deposits were found in India, then in Brazil in the eighteenth century, before the discovery of South African deposits in the late nineteenth century. Today, the main producers are Russia, Canada, and Botswana.

Cutting

Diamond cutting has evolved over the centuries. Until the fourteenth century, diamonds were mounted according to the natural shape of the raw stone, often an octahedron. This "point cut," in which

"Diamond," plate from *L'Encyclopédie Larousse*, 1933.
Illustrations of mines, cuts and shapes, industrial
applications, and famous diamonds

the sides are simply smoothed, was replaced by the "table cut" in the fifteenth century, where the point of the octahedron was sawn off to form a small, flat top. Gradually, facets began to be cut around the table and on the pavilion (the stone's lower part). In the same period, over the course of the sixteenth century, the "rose cut" was developed, characterized by triangular facets forming a dome with a flat base. The number of facets varied from three to twenty-four. This type of cut was in use until the beginning of the twentieth century, and is today back in fashion.

On the basis of the complex forms of the "table cut," diamond cutting evolved in the seventeenth century toward the ancestor of the "brilliant cut": the "brilliant old cut," usually known today in France simply as the "old cut." Historians cannot agree on the identity of this cut's creator. It seems that several diamond cutters, all observing the optical effects of certain forms, gradually brought about this remarkable cut. With fifty-eight facets, it has a high crown (upper part) and a deep pavilion (lower part). The culet or tip of the pavilion is usually flattened, thus forming the fifty-eighth facet. The "old cut" would evolve until the early twentieth century, from a square shape with rounded corners to a rounder cut.

The early twentieth century saw the development of the *demi-taille* (half-cut), similar in its proportions to the "modern cut." It usually retained the flattened pavilion tip. Although it was still commonly used in the 1930s, it was a transitional cut; it was superseded by the "modern brilliant cut," which was developed around 1910 and became popular several decades later. With fifty-seven facets, the "modern brilliant cut" reflected all of the light inside the gem from the table or the facets of the crown. To this effect, the pavilion was not as deep in relation to the diameter of the stone, the flattened culet disappeared, and the table was larger.

There are also "fancy" faceted cuts, including navette or marquise, pear, oval, heart, emerald, triangle, and baguette.

Today, the main diamond-cutting centers are primarily in India, but also in China and Africa (Botswana and Namibia). The largest stones are still cut in Belgium (Antwerp), Israel (Tel Aviv), and the United States (New York). The leading diamond exchanges are Antwerp, Dubai, and New York, followed by Hong Kong, Mumbai, and Tel Aviv.

Care

Diamond is characterized by its hardness, but it can still be scratched by another diamond. Care must also be taken to avoid knocks that might chip the ridges of the gem. Unlike most gemstones, diamond can withstand high temperatures. It can be immersed in boiling water with a little soap to remove grease, which diamond has a tendency to attract naturally.

"Toi et moi" or "vous et moi" (you-and-me) ring, late nineteenth century • gold and platinum, old-cut and rose-cut diamonds

Tortoiseshell

Characteristics

Tortoiseshell, which is often used in antique jewelry, is an organic material that comes from the shell of sea turtles. It is made of keratin, just like horn, nails, and hair. Unlike mineral materials, it can burn. The most sought-after tortoiseshell came from the hawksbill sea turtle (*Eretmochelys imbricata*). Used since antiquity, tortoiseshell was prized for its aesthetic qualities and for its many possible transformations. It was also used to make veneer for furniture and other objects.

History

Due to the extremely thermoplastic nature of tortoiseshell, it softens in boiling water and can then be worked or inlaid. Several pieces can be joined together by this means, placed in a mold and pressed to produce small toiletry items. Because of the trade in hawksbill turtle shell, this species is now in danger of extinction and is protected by the CITES (Convention on International Trade in Endangered Species of Wild Fauna and Flora); the international commercial trade of hawksbill turtles and their parts has been banned since 1977. However, in several countries, such as Japan, the domestic trade is legal and still continues.

While the sale of tortoiseshell is prohibited in many countries, certain antique pieces can be exempt, depending on the age and provenance of the item. These pieces must meet specific and stringent criteria, and the necessary exemption documentation, including proof of age and legal acquisition, is required.

Color(s)

Tortoiseshell exists in many different shades, ranging from pale yellow or translucent amber-yellow to dark brown.

Provenance

The hawksbill sea turtle is found in most tropical, subtropical, and even temperate regions.

Hair comb by Émile Froment-Meurice, c. 1880 • gold, tortoiseshell

"Négligé" necklace, c. 1910 •
platinum, emeralds, diamonds

Emerald

Characteristics

Emerald is a variety of beryl. It takes its name from the Greek *smaragdos* and the Latin *smaralda*, meaning "green stone." Emerald is rarely clear, because of the presence of inclusions, which are sometimes poetically called the *jardin* (French for "garden").

History

The popularity of emeralds has never waned, except briefly during the art nouveau period and in the 1940s. Most jewelry houses have used this gemstone. In the early twentieth century, the Indian princes commissioned Parisian jewelers to remount their gems, notably emeralds. At the 1925 Exposition Internationale des Arts Décoratifs et Industriels Modernes, Cartier presented the impressive 141.13-carat Bérénice Emerald.

Color(s)

The color of emerald ranges from yellow-green to blue-green. It has a velvety hue, attributed to the presence of chromium and vanadium.

Provenance

Emerald is not a widespread gemstone. Deposits in Egypt were mined in the first millennium BCE, and were taken over successively by the Greeks, the Romans, and the Turks. They were rediscovered by the French explorer Frédéric Cailliaud in 1816. Colombia emeralds were predominant in the sixteenth century in Europe, although the Native Indians had known of these deposits well before the arrival of the Spanish conquistadors. The Chivor mine was worked from 1545 and the Muzo mine from 1560. Since 1830, very fine emeralds have been found in Russia, specifically in the Urals. Brazil has been mining emeralds since 1913, and the African continent became a leading emerald producer from 1925, particularly Zambia and Zimbabwe.

Care

Emerald requires special care. It is fragile because of its inclusions, and is sensitive to strong temperature changes and to knocks. It is best to avoid ultrasonic cleaning methods and to use distilled water.

Garnet

Characteristics

The term "garnet" corresponds to a large mineral family of various colors and chemical compositions. Known since antiquity, the stone is mentioned in the writings of Greek philosopher Theophrastus, who called it "anthrax." The name "garnet" appeared around 1270; it comes from the Latin *granatus*, meaning "having seeds" or "having grains," in reference to the red seeds of the pomegranate. Red-colored pyrope and almandine are the most commonly used forms of garnet in jewelry. Green garnet, demantoid, was used in pavé settings in the late nineteenth century.

History

Garnet was very fashionable throughout the nineteenth century, particularly stones from Bohemia (Czech Republic). In France, garnet from the Eastern Pyrenees was popular from the nineteenth century until World War I thanks to the discovery of almandine deposits. Perpignan was the center of this jewelry trade. Some of its production was even exported to Algeria and Spain.

Color(s)

Garnet has a wide variety of colors. Pyrope garnet is deep red and almandine ranges from brownish-red to purplish-red. There are also orange, brown, and even green garnets.

Provenance

The garnet family is relatively widespread in the world. Deposits are found notably in Sri Lanka, Madagascar, Brazil, and India, as well as in Europe.

Earrings, c. 1860 • gold, enamel, garnets, natural pearls

Pendant designed
by Eugène Grasset for
jeweler Vever, c. 1900 •
gold, enamel, ivory

Ivory

Characteristics

Ivory (composed of calcium phosphate, like vertebrate bones and teeth) traditionally refers to elephant tusks. By extension, the term is also used for the tusks of other mammals, such as the hippopotamus, walrus, narwhal, boar, and mammoth, but the ivory's origin is always specified. Ivory has been used since prehistory for making objects, and every civilization has worked this precious material.

History

France opened a first trading post in Senegal in 1628, after which a bustling trade in ivory developed in the port of Dieppe. Ivory was unloaded from ships under royal charter and sent directly to the ivory dealers' shops. In the eighteenth century, there were some three hundred of these in the town. The July Monarchy (1830–1848) saw a resurgence of interest in ivory, which continued until the early twentieth century.

Today, ivory trading is subject to strict regulations according to the CITES (Convention on International Trade in Endangered Species of Wild Fauna and Flora), which fundamentally banned the international commercial trade of ivory. However, there are complex exceptions for antique pieces in ivory, depending on the age and composition of the artifact in question, and these exemptions vary from country to country. These pieces must be declared on sale or purchase, and the proper documentation provided.

Color(s)

Ivory is a cream/off-white color with an opaque appearance. It can be dyed. Ivory can react to cosmetics and dry out, and cracks may form. Its color can change from white to a brownish-yellow.

Brooch by Cartier, c. 1925 •
platinum, jadeite jade,
diamonds, sapphires,
rock crystal

Jade (jadeite and nephrite)

Characteristics

The term "jade" does not refer to a specific stone but to two similarly colored minerals, which are often green: jadeite and nephrite. Originally, the two stones were not differentiated. The name "jade" goes back to the time of the Spanish discovery of the Americas. It meant "kidney stone" or "stone of the flank" (*piedra de ijada* in Spanish), because it was believed to cure colic. This name became *pierre de l'éjade* in French, then "jade" in 1612. Later, it was given the scientific name *lapis nephriticus* from the Greek *nephros*, meaning "kidney," by analogy with the natural kidney-like shape of the pebbles containing nephrite jade. Translators rendered this as "nephritic stone," which became "nephrite." In 1863, the mineralogist Alexis Damour described nephrite jade and distinguished it from jadeite jade.

History

The use of jadeite jade dates back to the sacking of the Summer Palace in Peking during the 1860 French-British expedition to China. The jeweler Eugène Fontenay made pendants and earrings from the stone. This jade was also used in art deco designs, notably in bold combinations with onyx.

Color(s)

Jadeite with a luminous emerald-green color known as "imperial green" is highly sought after. However, the stone also exists in other hues, including yellow, white, lavender, and black. Nephrite, on the other hand, comes in every shade of green, albeit less bright, and it can also be gray-white or yellow. The green color is due to the presence of chromium (in "imperial jade") and iron.

Provenance

Jadeite is rare. There are ten to twelve deposits in the world, notably in Myanmar (Burma), Japan, and Guatemala. Nephrite is found in New Zealand, Australia, Brazil, Canada, and China.

Jet

Characteristics

Jet is a product of the carbonization of ancient wood in a swampy environment, followed by a natural compression process. It was known and used as early as the second millennium BCE in England.

History

The assassination of the Duke of Berry on February 13, 1820, and the death of Louis XVIII four years later developed the market for mourning jewelry, which continued until the early twentieth century. After a death, the rules of etiquette were strict. There were three periods: during the full, or deep, mourning, no jewelry could be worn; during second mourning, black jewelry and hair ornaments were permitted; and during half mourning, gold was allowed. Fashion journals reported on the subject: "Black jewelry is all the rage: jet, iron, and any composition in black are worn in every form. Jeweler's shops now all seem to be devoted to mourning." Queen Victoria's long widowhood, which lasted almost forty years, bolstered the phenomenon, making the most of the large jet deposit in Whitby, in Yorkshire (United Kingdom). In France, the *Annuaire Azur* business directory of 1862 lists fifty-four jewelers specialized in mourning jewelry. However, owing to the rarity and relative softness of this material, French jewelers often used "French jet" or "Parisian jet": a black glass with purplish edges.

Color(s)

This lightweight material is black in color with a brilliant luster.

Provenance

The main deposits are in Yorkshire, United Kingdom, and in northeastern Spain.

Necklace,
nineteenth century • gold, jet

Lapis Lazuli

Characteristics

Lapis lazuli is a blue rock made up of several different minerals. Its name comes from the Latin *lapis* ("stone") and the Medieval Latin *lazuli*, derived from the Arabic *lazaward*, from the Persian *lazhuward* ("azure").

History

Lapis lazuli has been used since the earliest antiquity. In Egypt, it was considered a sacred stone, evocative of the starry sky. Lapis lazuli was introduced to Europe in the fifth century. It was popular in the art deco period.

Color(s)

The dominant and highly-prized color of this rock is a deep blue. Lapis lazuli can be flecked with pyrite crystals and feature white veins of calcite. When crushed, it produces a precious ultramarine blue pigment, which was synthesized in 1826.

Provenance

The famous historic site of Sar-i Sang in Afghanistan has been mined since antiquity and was mentioned by Marco Polo. In Russia, a deposit was discovered in 1797 during an expedition organized by Empress Catherine II. Other deposits are located in Pakistan, Tajikistan, Chile, the United States, and Myanmar (Burma).

Earrings by Eugène Fontenay, 1867/1882 • gold, lapis lazuli

Pendant, c. 1930 •
platinum and gold, onyx, diamonds

Onyx

Characteristics
Onyx is a variety of chalcedony (microcrystalline silica). Its name comes from the ancient Greek *ónyx*, meaning "nail" or "claw," because of its layered structure. Since antiquity, it has been used notably for making cameos and intaglio carvings.

History
In the nineteenth century, onyx was often used in mourning jewelry, owing to its color. In the art deco period, it was combined with coral or jade.

Color(s)
Onyx is black or has alternating bands of black and white.

Provenance
Onyx is found mainly in Brazil, Mexico, the United States, and Uruguay.

Opal

Characteristics

The term "opal" covers a range of minerals made up of hydrated silica. Its name is thought to come from the Sanskrit *upala*, meaning "precious stone." There are two main types of opal: precious or noble opal, the most highly sought after, which is characterized by its iridescence or intense play-of-color; and common opal, which is usually opaque or translucent with a single color and no luster. For some, opal serves as a talisman, while others consider it bad luck, believing it to cause accidents, or even death.

History

Opal has always been appreciated, as shown by the discovery of a six-thousand-year-old opal in a cave in Kenya in 1932 by the anthropologist Louis Leakey. Emperor Napoleon I gave Joséphine an opal named the Incendie de Troie (Burning of Troy), featuring a magnificent display of colors; no one knows what became of it. Empress Eugénie, on the other hand, was afraid of opal. Art nouveau designers, not least René Lalique, made use of the stone's iridescent reflections in highly creative pieces.

Color(s)

The basic colors of opal are white, gray, blue, green, orange, and black. Its play-of-colors is due to interferences of light.

Provenance

In the past, opals came from Egypt and Slovakia. Today, the largest deposits are in Australia and have been mined since the late nineteenth century. Opals are also found in Brazil, Mexico, the United States, and Ethiopia.

Care

Opal is sensitive to changes in temperature; it contains water and can become dehydrated. Where possible, opal should not be kept in an environment that is too dry.

Ring, late nineteenth century • gold, opal, diamonds

Pair of large ear clips by René Boivin,
c. 1950 • gold and platinum, natural
pearls, diamonds

Pearl (natural and cultured)

Characteristics

There are two types of pearl: natural or
"fine" pearls and cultured pearls. Natural
pearls form without human intervention
in certain mollusks, usually oysters and
gastropods, in the nacre-secreting mantle
tissue. In the past, free divers would
harvest the oysters and occasionally find
a pearl. Cultured pearls require human
intervention: a small nucleus bead of
nacre with a piece of mantle tissue from
a sacrificed oyster are implanted in the

oyster's reproductive organ (gonad);
secreted layers of nacre will cover the
shell bead.

The sought-after characteristics of
pearls are their "orient" (the optical
phenomenon of iridescence), luster, and
color. Cultured pearls became highly
popular from the late 1920s in France,
but their history dates back further.
Experiments with pearls have been carried
out since the twelfth century; tiny mother-
of-pearl buddhas were made by inserting

buddhas made of lead or tin into mollusks. In 1761, the Swede Carl Linnaeus managed to produce a few cultured pearls, which are today held at the British Museum. Drawing on this work, the Japanese—in particular Kokichi Mikimoto—developed the production of spherical cultured pearls in seawater, around 1920. Tahiti pearls are cultured pearls produced by black-lip oysters. Today, the Chinese produce freshwater cultured pearls in a mold, without a nacre nucleus.

History

One of the oldest known pearls fished by humans is the Jomon pearl, which is about 5,500 years old and was found in Japan on an archeological site from the Jomon civilization. According to recent archeological discoveries, pearls were fished in Mesopotamia as early as the third millennium BCE. The first document recording this practice was written by the Greek historian Megasthenes.

Natural pearls were in great demand during the Renaissance and in the nineteenth century. Through the nineteenth century, the graduated necklace was in fashion, with a larger pearl in the center and progressively smaller pearls on either side. By the late nineteenth and early twentieth centuries, strong demand had pushed up prices. From the 1920s onward, cultured pearls became more affordable and were a great commercial success.

Color(s)

Although it is usually pinkish-white, a pearl's color depends on the species of oyster and the trace elements present in the water.

Provenance

The main fishing locations for natural pearls were in the Persian Gulf, in Sri Lanka (formerly Ceylon), and in Japan. Many rivers yielded natural pearls, notably in Scotland, Sweden, and the United States. In France, pearls of the Vologne were harvested until the early twentieth century. In 1806, the town of Plombières presented Empress Joséphine with a pearl bracelet. The twentieth century saw the development of cultured-pearl farming techniques all over the world, particularly in Polynesia and in China, where saltwater and freshwater pearls respectively are cultivated.

Care

Great care must be taken with pearls. They are particularly sensitive to heat and acidic substances, so contact with perspiration or perfume should be avoided. They should not remain enclosed in a box for too long. They can be cleaned with a soft, damp cloth. Regular restringing of a necklace is recommended to prevent strand breakage and to avoid acidic substances being absorbed into the pearls through capillary action. Because pearls are not very hard, they should not be worn with stones that might scratch them.

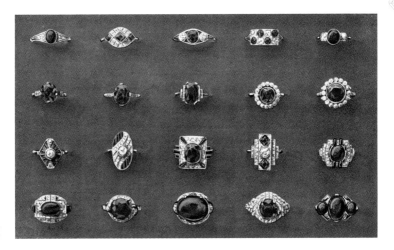

Ruby rings,
Dusausoy catalog, 1929

Ruby

Characteristics

Ruby belongs to the corundum (aluminum oxide) family of gemstones. It owes its name to its red color, from the Latin *ruber*. Indians gave it the Sanskrit name *ratnanayaka*, meaning "lord of gemstones." Ruby has been known since the first millennium BCE, but it remained very rare through antiquity. The stones are generally small in size; gems with a very fine color rarely exceed 4 carats.

History

Ruby is a rare gemstone. In the nineteenth century, the supply increased in France when rubies from Burma began to be imported in 1856, then from Siam (present-day Thailand) in 1861.

Color(s)

Ruby's color varies from bright red to dark, purplish-red or raspberry red. The "pigeon blood" color—a dark shade of crimson—is the most sought after. The depth of a ruby's color depends on the amount of chromium present.

Provenance

For many years, the finest stones came from the Mogok Valley, in Burma (Myanmar), and the discovery of this deposit hidden deep in the jungle is steeped in legend. In Thailand, the commercial operating of mines began in the 1930s. Stones from Thailand and Cambodia were called "Siam rubies." Ruby is also found in Sri Lanka, Kenya, Tanzania, Mozambique, and Afghanistan.

Care

Rubies can be cleaned with soapy water.

Sapphire

Characteristics

Sapphire derives its name from the Greek *sappheiros*, referring to a blue-colored stone. Like ruby, sapphire is a variety of corundum (aluminum oxide). However, it is not as rare as ruby. Sapphire has been one of the most popular gemstones since around 800 BCE.

History

Sapphire has been used in jewelry continuously throughout history. The sapphire-encrusted parure of Marie-Amélie, queen of Louis-Philippe, which is held today in the Musée du Louvre, was successively expanded and reworked. The arrival of numerous Australian sapphires on the market in the late nineteenth century—and in even larger quantities after World War I—broadened the supply. But the most sought after and rarest sapphires are Kashmir sapphires, discovered in the late nineteenth century, with their unique, velvety cobalt blue color.

Color(s)

Sapphire's blue ranges from light to dark, but the gemstone can appear in every color, and can even be colorless. Its blue hue is due to the presence of iron and titanium, which may be spread unevenly through the stone. The padparadscha ("lotus flower" in Sinhalese) sapphire is pink-orange.

Provenance

Sapphire is fairly widespread in the world. In Sri Lanka (formerly Ceylon), where the stone often has an attractive, light color, it has been mined since antiquity. The deposits in Burma (Myanmar) yield magnificent deep blue stones, while those in Thailand and Cambodia are highly productive but produce stones with less remarkable colors. The Anakie fields in Queensland, Australia, were discovered in 1870; their sapphires are much darker. Finally, the most renowned deposits, in Kashmir, at an altitude of over 13,000 feet (4,000 m), began to be mined in the late nineteenth century.

Care

Sapphires can be cleaned with soapy water.

Ring by Suzanne Belperron, c. 1938 • gold and platinum, sapphire cabochon, diamonds

Pair of bracelets attributed
to Mellerio, July Monarchy
period • gold, turquoises,
pearls, two miniatures on
ivory depicting Louis-Philippe
and Marie-Amélie

Turquoise

Characteristics

Turquoise has been used for ornamental
purposes since antiquity. Its name appeared
in the thirteenth century. The gem was
believed to come from Turkey; in fact, it
was mined in Persia but transited through
Turkey, where it was bought and sold.

History

The vogue for all things Egyptian in the
Second Empire (1852–1870) brought
turquoise back into fashion. The stone
remained popular in the art nouveau and
art deco styles. Turquoise was also used in
the 1950s, notably in the pieces produced
by the jeweler Pierre Sterlé.

Color(s)

The colors of turquoise range from pale
blue to green, and are due to the presence
of copper and iron.

Provenance

Deposits were mined in Egypt in the Sinai
as far back as the Old Kingdom period
(c. 2700–2200 BCE). Today, turquoise
gemstones come from Iran, Tibet, China,
Mexico, and the United States.

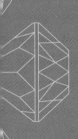

Main Types
of Jewelry

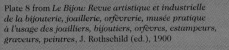

Plate 8 from *Le Bijou: Revue artistique et industrielle de la bijouterie, joaillerie, orfèvrerie, musée pratique à l'usage des joailliers, bijoutiers, orfèvres, estampeurs, graveurs, peintres*, J. Rothschild (ed.), 1900

Ring, c. 1940 • gold, diamonds

Ring

Since the dawn of time, the ring has been one of the most common forms of jewelry, worn by women and men alike. The earliest rings were made of bone or ivory, sometimes with an ornamental stone. Besides its decorative aspect, a ring can play a utilitarian role as a sign of recognition, with a social or religious function. It can also have sentimental significance, such as an engagement or wedding ring. There are numerous different models but they are all forms of either the bezel ring or the signet ring. The former has a raised top part which may hold a stone, a small carving, or a motif in enamel, while the latter has a wide, flat bezel, in metal or with an ornamental stone, sometimes engraved with initials, a coat of arms, or an emblem.

Consulate and First Empire

Under the First Empire, rings inspired by antiquity featured cameos, intaglios, and scarabs. Others with a pivoting bezel carried miniature scenes or sentimental symbols. The imperial family gave many rings as gifts. A popular design was the puzzle ring, made up of several interlocking bands, each set with a different stone whose initial letters, when combined correctly, formed a person's name or a word.

Restoration and July Monarchy

Under the Restoration and the July Monarchy, rings were often in enameled gold, and were delicate in appearance and execution. They were sometimes sentimental, for example with an envelope-shaped bezel opening onto an enameled heart or an inscription. Fede rings with two hands intertwined, worn as engagement rings, were also in vogue. Commemorative rings continued to be made, in memory of the Duke of Berry or the Emperor Napoleon, whose face might appear in a small open coffin depicted on the bezel.

Second Empire and Late Nineteenth Century

Under the Second Empire, rings were often larger, less romantic, and more traditional, and usually featured a center stone and bezel. In the mid-nineteenth century, Oscar Massin invented a bezel setting that made the stone look larger. In 1886, Tiffany mounted the diamond in a solitaire setting, held detached from the band with six prongs. Men often wore signet rings and engraved rings in the neo-Renaissance style.

Belle Époque

Belle Époque rings were classic in style and set with diamonds, sapphires, emeralds, rubies, or pearls. The most common models were the "toi et moi" or "vous et moi" (you-and-me) ring, comprising two gemstones of the same size mounted side by side, and the "tourbillon" ring, in which the central stone was surrounded by a swirl of smaller stones.

Art Nouveau

Rings were less frequently worn during the art nouveau period. The bezel and band did not provide enough scope for the jeweler's imagination. The rare specimens that exist feature fluid curves expressed through intertwined bodies, loose hair, and plant motifs.

Art Deco

Platinum rings embraced the full diversity of art deco, from geometric compositions to stylized floral motifs. In 1929, *Harper's Bazaar* described the trend: "The fashionable *Parisienne* wears a wedding ring in the form of a band of diamonds, and a large solitaire, and perhaps another large colored ring, usually holding a single stone—an emerald, turquoise, or sapphire—to match the color of her dress."

1940s

In the 1940s, yellow-gold rings were voluminous and striking, and generally set with small stones, which were sometimes synthetic. Models included the "bridge," "open-book," "Turkish," "turban," "tent," and "knot" rings.

1950s

In the 1950s, rings came in many variations. They were reminiscent of 1940s designs, but lighter in spirit and more boldly colored, combining amethyst, turquoise, diamond, or citrine. The bezel was often raised.

Rings from the late nineteenth century to the 1950s

Earrings

According to records, jewelry has been worn on the ears since antiquity, by both women and men. Earrings are usually fastened through a hole pierced in the earlobe, but certain models can be screwed or clipped onto the ear.

Consulate and First Empire

Earrings in this period reflected the influence of antiquity. "Greek" hairstyles worn during this time exposed the ears and neck. Long earrings came back into fashion in the First Empire, studded with cameos, pearls, or precious stones, matching the tiara, belt, and necklace in court parures. For everyday use, large, lightweight earrings worn with loose, flowing garments were made up of flat motifs linked together with side chains suspended from the earlobe by a hook. The "poissarde" earring, for example, with a semicircular or S-shaped wire, held a long oval motif made up of rows of small stones or enameled plates. The name is thought to come from a play staged in 1797: *Madame Angot, ou la Poissarde parvenue* by Antoine-François Ève, also known as Demaillot. A crude and vulgar woman was called a poissarde, or "fishwife," and the term "Madame Angot" began to be used for a working-class woman with newly acquired wealth who kept her rough manners and speech. Others believe that the term derives from the long earrings worn by fishwives themselves.

Restoration and July Monarchy

Under the Restoration and in the early days of the July Monarchy, long earrings were an integral part of a woman's parure. Lightweight and fragile, they were made of embossed or repoussé gold, sometimes with filigree work or granulation (granules of gold). Added to this metal were colored hardstones such as amethyst, citrine, and aquamarine. In the 1840s, this type of jewelry disappeared when a new hairstyle became popular, in which the hair was divided into bands that completely covered the ears.

Second Empire and Late Nineteenth Century

Earrings gradually came back into fashion. In the early 1870s, relatively simple ear studs began to evolve into long pendants—sometimes over four inches (10 cm) long. New hairstyles exposed the ears; fastenings improved. In 1855, a certain M. Billiet filed a patent for *dormeuses*, or sleepers, in Paris. These small, compact drop earrings could be kept in at night. The hook came through the earlobe from the back and blocked at the top. Their motifs become more varied, inspired by nature, antiquity, the Renaissance, and, later, India, China, and Japan. They were sometimes boldly eccentric, such as a design with small brooding hens in a basket suspended on three small chains attached to the hook, or another with violins, or one with two buckets attached to a pulley, created by Eugène Fontenay.

Belle Époque and Art Nouveau

After 1880, earrings were worn less often, despite the fashion for chignons, which exposed the ears. Earrings were plainer in design, often in the form of studs with diamonds and pearls. The star and crescent moon motifs that had appeared in the 1860s became more common. Diamond drop earrings in the "garland" style were worn from 1900, and the same period saw the development of screw fastenings. Art nouveau designers showed little interest in earrings, however.

Art Deco

The fashion for cropped hair lent itself well to long drop earrings in platinum, with a vertical, geometric line and contrasting colors. Long drops of coral and jadeite jade were combined with small diamonds and onyx, fastened to the earlobe with a screw-back mechanism,

or, better still, a safety push-back clasp. In the 1930s, earrings became heavier and wider, gradually growing bolder and more voluminous. Designs were studded with colored stones and diamonds of all sizes. For women who did not wish to have their ears pierced, clip-ons made their appearance, with a clasp at the back of the earring hidden behind the rounded front motif: rosettes, spirals, whirls, and waves in diamonds thus sat perfectly on the earlobe.

1940s

Earrings, often in the form of studs, broke with the styles of the 1930s. Among the varied themes were volutes, bows, and flowers and buds, studded with natural or synthetic diamonds or rubies. Drop earrings were rarer, carrying clusters of small stones, ribbons, or gold chains. Clip-on earrings were often in yellow gold, with few stones and a curving rather than geometric line.

1950s

Earring designs in the 1950s were very diverse, with fluid lines and sinuous shapes suggesting movement and lightness. Delicate gold trimmings in the form of chains, braiding, or tassels were often featured. Women wore their hair either long, in a chignon, or cut short. The majority of them no longer had their ears pierced, preferring clip-on studs or drops, which were quick and easy to change. Day earrings were in gold, while evening earrings were more often in platinum or white gold. Diamonds and pearls were popular.

"Poissarde" earrings, early nineteenth century • gold, enamel

Pair of bracelets, c. 1930 • platinum, natural pearls, diamonds

Bracelet

The bracelet is an item of jewelry most often worn on the wrist, but it can also be worn on the arm, above the elbow, or on the ankle. It may be rigid, when made out of a single piece of metal, semirigid with moving parts, or flexible with chains and links. This section deals with arm and wrist bracelets.

Consulate and First Empire

During the First Empire, Greco-Roman-style dresses left the arms bare. Bracelets, worn in pairs on the wrist and sometimes on the upper arm, formed part of the outfit. These jewelry pieces were flexible, articulated, and comprised decorative elements—gemstones, fragile chased gold leaves, several rows of pearls, small chains linking cameos, or lockets containing hair. The clasp sometimes echoed the bracelet's motif. Personalized puzzle bracelets were made up of a row of gemstones, whose initial letters spelled a word or name.

Restoration and July Monarchy

Under the Restoration, bracelets were much larger and lighter, and they were an essential element of any parure. In the 1820s and 1830s, these often fragile pieces were made using sophisticated and intricate techniques: filigree (thin, threadlike strips of metal that are twisted or woven), gold cannetille (similar to filigree but with three-dimensional ornaments, such as twisted coils), and granulation (small beads of precious metal used to decorate and form a design), sometimes studded with large colored gemstones. The 1840s saw the emergence of heavy neo-Gothic and neo-Renaissance bracelets in silver that was deliberately oxidized, as well as bracelets in gold that were hollow, articulated, or enameled, featuring ribbon, bow, or tree branch motifs. A popular design was the "bird defending its nest from a snake."

Second Empire
and Late Nineteenth Century

The bracelet was a favorite item of jewelry in the Second Empire. Although the pieces were increasingly voluminous and eclectic in design, the custom was to layer or stack several on each arm. Relatively lightweight but large-sized models in gold came in a variety of shapes and inspirations: wide, hinged designs, which were engraved, enameled, or encrusted with faceted or cabochon gems, featuring a cameo, a miniature portrait, or a large sapphire circled by diamonds; heavy cuff bracelets, in the shape of a truncated cone or with moving enameled plates; and bracelets with drop beads, pendants, or small chains. Motifs were Greco-Roman, neo-Gothic, neo-Renaissance, or naturalist. The snake bracelet was popular. Toward the end of the century, bracelets became narrower, sometimes made of gold-encrusted steel, with a motto in Gothic lettering in cloisonné enamel.

Art Nouveau
Bracelets in the art nouveau style are very rare. The few examples were often enameled and in relief, and were made of materials that were not very resistant to knocks and scratches.

Art Deco
With the fashion for bare arms, bracelets were back—in vast numbers. In the 1920s, several were worn on each arm, on the wrist and in pairs on the upper arm. They were often of Byzantine, Oriental, Egyptian, or Asian inspiration. There were models encrusted with colored gemstones, onyx, and diamonds, or comprised of several rows of pearls. Motifs were symmetrical and geometric. In the early 1930s, several were still worn on the wrist, but they were larger and made of platinum and diamonds with articulated motifs. Supple like a fabric, flexible, or rigid and heavy, they resembled elements of architecture. Toward the end of this period, they were often in yellow gold, sometimes combined with green or rose, almost red, gold, and studded with topazes, rubies, or sapphires.

1940s
The highly characteristic bracelets from this period were wide, articulated, or rigid. Motifs were square, rectangular, hexagonal, round, or trapezoid. Gold "tank" bracelets—thus named because of their articulated links resembling a tank's caterpillar tracks—were in vogue. Some bracelet designs were flexible, with a "snake" or "tubogas" (gas-tube) chain; others were supple, such as the broad, flat ribbon design composed of small hexagonal or staggered rectangular motifs that were articulated, which was inspired by the Van Cleef & Arpels Ludo bracelet from 1934 and 1935. Gemstones set in bracelets were generally small in size, and included diamonds, rubies, sapphires, and synthetic stones, or larger citrines and amethysts.

1950s
The bracelet was an essential item of jewelry in the 1950s. Pieces had rounded reliefs and were suggestive of fabric trimmings or sewn items, with braided, twisted, or intertwined gold threads that were sometimes encrusted with small diamonds, or else ribbons of all sorts in gold, featuring woven, twill, or guilloché effects. These more supple designs could be adorned with small charms.

Brooch

A brooch is a jewelry piece with a pin held in place by a clasp, enabling it to be fastened to a garment or hat. The ancestor of the brooch—the fibula—originally served to close items of clothing. Brooches were worn by women and men from antiquity through the Middle Ages, and their utilitarian function gradually became purely ornamental.

Consulate and First Empire

Clothing inspired by ancient Greece was generally made of a fabric that was too thin to support a brooch. Nor was there space for a brooch on a dress whose belt under the bust was often adorned with pearls, gems, and cameos. Occasionally, however, one was worn at the top of the shoulder.

Restoration and July Monarchy

Brooches made a timid comeback around 1823, when they were placed at the center of a dress's low-cut bodice. They were common from 1835 onward, ornamented with colored gemstones and granulation or filigree work. When a brooch's principal motif was a gem, it might feature gold drop pendants or pearl drops. There were also neo-Gothic silver brooches, with angels and saints, and ivy or vine foliage, in enameled gold. More sophisticated brooches featured small suspended chains with spherical beads or hearts at their tips.

Second Empire and Late Nineteenth Century

During the Second Empire, more naturalistic brooches made an appearance, composed of flowers and leaves in diamonds and pearls; they often featured tassels, which could measure over eight inches (20 cm) in length. Other designs, worn vertically, formed sprays of wild roses, lily-of-the-valley, or cornflowers. To achieve a more realistic look, "tremblant" (trembling) brooches had flowers mounted on springs, which allowed them to sparkle with the slightest movement. In the same vein, Mellerio filed a patent for a mount on a flexible stem, to give suppleness to plant motifs. Bodice brooches sometimes featured a large central cameo and an enameled gold mount in the neo-Greek or neo-Renaissance style. Others had equestrian motifs, or were made of polished steel. By the end of the Empire period, highly realistic animal motifs had come to the fore, including butterflies, flies, grasshoppers, beetles, and lizards.

Belle Époque

Traditional jewelry included diamond-studded brooches in platinum in the shape of bows, arrows, clover leaves, flowers, crescent moons, and stars, which had already been seen in the Second Empire. From 1900 until the 1930s, the bar brooch became a popular design, featuring a line of stones or pearls, sometimes with suspended pear-drop pearls. The brooch could be transformed into a hair pin or a tiara ornament.

Art Nouveau

Art nouveau brooches were characterized mostly by their use of enamel, opal, ivory, and pearl. They featured plant motifs in enameled gold—plane tree, maple, fuchsia, nasturtium, orchid, etc.—as well as animals, including peacocks, butterflies, and dragonflies with transparent, iridescent wings. Lalique mounted engraved pressed glass on chased patinated silver.

Art Deco

Brooches were highly popular during this period. Colorful geometric motifs adorned collars, lapels, belts, headbands, or hats. Dress clips were widespread from the 1920s onward, becoming an item of jewelry that was typical of the 1930s. With a clip-style back—either a hinged-spring clip that "pinched" the fabric or a double-prong hinged clip with sharp ends that pierced the fabric like a pin—they could be worn alone, or, in the case of a double clip brooch, in a pair, on either side of the décolletage, for example; when put together, the pair formed a third, larger brooch. In the 1920s, a pearl-and-diamond or sapphire-and-diamond bar brooch would be pinned to the front of a hat. In the 1930s, a diamond pavé or carved gemstone clip was often fastened to a scarf, bag, glove, or bracelet. A brooch might also serve to close a coat. Hat brooches were long pins ornamented with colored stone balls, or a motif such as a butterfly, and used a wide variety of materials including natural or artificial stones, wood, metal, and horn. There were also brooches made of a band of onyx or frosted rock crystal, mounted with decorative motifs, often in diamonds.

1940s

Brooches and dress clips remained popular. Gold lace bow brooches were back in fashion, with diamonds set in platinum. Naturalistic motifs included floral bouquets set with small stones and tied with polished-gold ribbons or sprinkled with diamonds.

1950s

Dress clips were worn on the drape at the shoulder, on belts, on cuffs, and to attach gloves. Popular materials included gold, topaz, emerald, diamonds, or glass paste, and they were worn in a variety of ways: alone, in pairs, in threes, or even as a set of four on the décolletage of a bodice, in a row, or in different places on an outfit. Dress clips and brooches from these years were highly eclectic in style, featuring snowflake, flower, and animal motifs.

Brooch by Cartier, c. 1950 • gold and platinum, diamonds, sapphires, rubies, emeralds

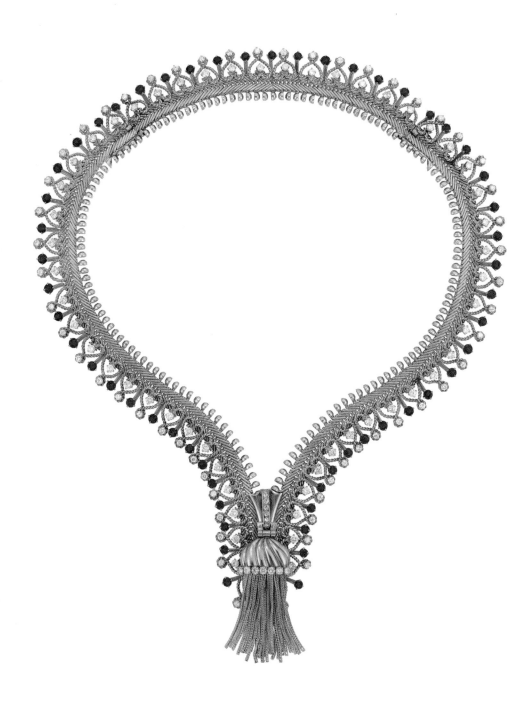

Zip necklace by Van Cleef & Arpels, c. 1955 • gold and platinum, rubies, diamonds

Necklace

This is one of the oldest forms of jewelry. Composed of a string of decorative elements to be worn around the neck, the necklace was originally made with shells, teeth, or fragments of bone. It has been continuously popular through the ages, in countless variations.

Consulate and First Empire

Under the influence of neoclassicism, necklaces drew inspiration from antiquity and featured cameos, micromosaics, and motifs in embossed and enameled gold rather than carved gems, which were few and far between. The decorative elements were often linked together with small chains of different styles and lengths. These were very delicately made and were called "esclavage" (slavery) necklaces. Long chains, known as "sautoirs," were also worn.

Restoration and July Monarchy

The necklace was an important element of parures. In the 1820s and 1830s, it was still worn "en esclavage," entirely in cannetille and granulation. Sometimes, these were set with citrines, amethysts, or aquamarines. A cross, heart, or other pendant might be suspended from a necklace made up of small enameled gold plates. Some necklaces featured differently colored cabochon and cut gemstones, in decreasing sizes. In the same period, long, lightweight sautoir chains in embossed and enameled gold were worn over the shoulders.

Second Empire and Late Nineteenth Century

Necklaces were very much in vogue during the Second Empire. Their inspirations were numerous and included neo-Greco-Roman gold pieces with palmettes, oat kernels, and amphorae; Campana or Cupid necklaces with two links falling over the back, forming angel wings; neo-Egyptian necklaces with enameled lotus flowers; Louis XV-style necklaces, like the Du Barry necklace in black velvet and jet; naturalistic necklaces featuring emerald insects with ruby eyes and diamond flowers; and neo-Renaissance-style designs. Others were more whimsical, such as the Gabrielle collar necklace with its gold garland undulating around the neck and rock-crystal drops suspended on small chains. Numerous variants exist, with drop beads or small chains, or a rose gold cable chain carrying a medallion, locket, or cross. A range of gemstones were used, including coral, turquoise, garnet, and diamond, as well as natural pearls (in multiple strands or a graduated string). After 1870, necklaces were worn over a high-necked bodice.

Belle Époque

In the late nineteenth century, there was a vogue for the dog-collar necklace, worn around the neck at the throat. Designs varied but generally entailed one central decorated plaque (*plaque de cou*), or several of them placed at regular intervals, attached to a ribbon or multiple rows of seed pearls or stones. They sometimes featured diamond motifs ornamented with colored gemstones. The fashion appears to have been started around 1880 by Alexandra, wife of King Edward VII, who wore this type of necklace to hide a scar. Sometimes the necklace was a single-strand choker of pearls, emeralds, or diamonds, or was decorated with garlands. Long pearl necklaces were often worn with these chokers. The Belle Époque "négligé" necklace terminated in an asymmetrical pair of pearl or diamond pendants, suspended on chains held by a small bar.

Art Nouveau

The art nouveau movement particularly appreciated the dog-collar necklace: the large decorated plaques provided plenty of scope for jewelers' fertile imagination, allowing them to compose sparkling landscapes depicting the metamorphoses of nature, using translucent enamels, gems, and colored glass. The "bayadère"—multiple strands of seed pearls twisted together into a long rope that was knotted at the chest—left the two ends of the necklace to hang free, ending in tassels or enameled plaques.

Art Deco

In the 1920s, many necklaces were strung with enormous beads of ivory, red coral, amber, jadeite jade, turquoise, and crystal, and tied around the neck with a velvet bow. Others hung down to the waist. The sautoir was in fashion: long flexible chains encrusted with stones on platinum, in geometric motifs, adorned the décolletage and the top of the back. In the 1930s, the necklace evolved from a supple chain to a collar of gems, sometimes with a bow motif or intertwined ribbons of faceted rubies and diamonds. Necklaces were also made of hardstones, in gold-, chrome-, or silver-plated metal.

1940s

Necklaces were worn close to the neck. The "snake" or "tubogas" (gas-tube) chain was in vogue, as was the thinner "rat tail" version. Gold snake chains could be wrapped around the neck and held in place with floral clips of sophisticated design, with a groove for the chain to pass through. Other examples of this type of chain featured a bow motif in front. Necklaces with medallions and twisted strands of pearls were also popular.

1950s

It is hard to pinpoint one particular style of necklace that was fashionable in the 1950s, as many different designs were produced. Numerous models were inspired by fabric trimmings, with chains of braided or twisted gold held together with a floral motif at the neck. A chain might be worn like a bayadère with a clip. Other pieces featured a fringe of gold thread resembling a frayed ribbon, or a cascade of faceted diamonds on white gold.

Pendant

A pendant is an ornament worn around the neck, suspended from a chain or necklace, usually by means of a jump ring. A pendant might be a medallion or locket, a cross, a charm, or other object.

Consulate and First Empire

Pendants were mostly sentimental and were delicate in design. The miniature portrait of a loved one might be visible on the outside, while on the back, a lock of hair could be worked to form the lovers' initials. Other miniatures and works in hair represented altars of love, floral bouquets, or pierced hearts.

Restoration and July Monarchy

Pendants remained sentimental in theme, featuring a miniature portrait, or a heart in filigree circled by a snake and containing a lock of hair. Small objects were suspended on a chain, such as a little golden key, a pencil holder, an enameled scent flask, and various types of cross.

Second Empire and Late Nineteenth Century

From the mid-nineteenth century, pendants included all kinds of medallions or lockets, crosses, and charms—with or without drop beads—which could be attached to a necklace or at the end of a chain. Often oval in shape, medallions drew on a variety of inspirations: they evoked antiquity, with cameos, micromosaics, and amphorae; the Renaissance, with enameled scroll mounts; the Louis XV and Louis XVI styles, with shepherdess miniatures framed in pearls; or the Japanese mode, with cloisonné enamels of kingfishers, roosters, chrysanthemums, and cherry blossoms. Lockets were very popular until the late nineteenth century. Made of gold, they were engraved, encrusted with pearls or turquoises, and featured niello decoration (a technique using a black alloy) or were often enameled in black. They enclosed a miniature portrait or photograph, sometimes with a lock of hair. Some were of sophisticated design: inside the locket, two portraits could be inserted into a glass holder in the center, while two more could be placed inside each side of the case. The Second Empire also saw the development of transformable jewelry. A medallion might be transformed into a brooch, for example.

Art Nouveau

The art nouveau movement also adopted pendants, but they no longer opened up to contain a sentimental memento: they became decorative items in their own right, to be exhibited. Their design was now defined by the form of the motif rather than by a geometric framework. Made of enameled or chased gold, sometimes set with a central gem or an ivory carving, pendants took up the popular themes of the art nouveau style: the female figure, flora, and fauna.

Art Deco

The pendant was one of the most characteristic jewelry pieces of the art deco period. "It adds a note of color that completes the effect of one's outfit," wrote a journalist in *Vogue* in 1921. Simple, geometric in form, and suspended from a long chain, it might be an oval in crystal, framed and encrusted with flowers and leaves; a round ring of black onyx dotted with small diamonds, hanging from a "rat tail" chain; or else rectangular, held and framed by a cord with a silk tassel. Designs in jade—often carved—were of Chinese inspiration, while other motifs were drawn from Indian iconography. In the 1930s, pendants were larger and more stylized, often featuring a central stone. They might also take the form of jets of water falling in a cascade of diamonds and colored gemstones. Pendants were worn on a matching short and flexible necklace.

1940s and 1950s

Pendants fell out of favor during this period. However, charms—small jewelry pieces attached to a bracelet or, more rarely, a chain—were in fashion.

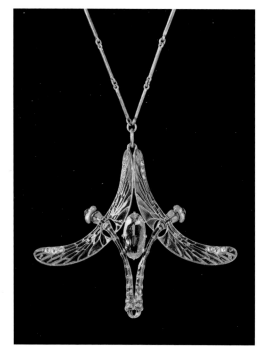

Dragonfly pendant by René Lalique, c. 1900 • gold, enamel, aquamarine, diamonds

Head Ornament

The jeweled headpiece is an ornament worn mostly by women. Several types of head ornament are derived from the crown, such as the bandeau tiara and the aigrette, which is shaped like a bird's plume. Head ornaments go back to antiquity, and continued to be reinvented until the early twentieth century. Another type of headpiece is the hair ornament, such as the comb, pin, and slide. Combs were an essential hair accessory in the nineteenth century.

Consulate and First Empire

During this period, the tiara or diadem, which was a constituent element of the parure, was usually worn in the evening and for official occasions. The *Journal des dames et des modes* of 15 Nivôse, year XII (January 6, 1804) described the custom: "The most fashionable coiffure for women remains the Etruscan or Greek style. No ornament and no hat hiding the hair, but a diadem adorning the forehead is indispensable; it should now be worn lower on one side than on the other, and the latest diadems in gold, silver, or cannetille, with either a cameo or a star, a rose, or a carnation, extend around the head to form at once a diadem and a crown." Under the First Empire, women would also wear a large comb on the top of their head to hold a chignon in place, its curved surface usually ornamented with coral beads, or sometimes with cameos or micromosaics.

Restoration and the July Monarchy

The tiara formed part of most aristocratic families' jewelry collection. As the most prominent piece of the wedding attire, it elevated the rank of the woman wearing it. Tiaras with cannetille and filigree work displayed large citrines, amethysts, or aquamarines. The naturalistic influence was predominant, with "Greek-style" tiaras composed of primroses and white lilac. Hair ornaments were sprinkled with diamonds, in tiaras adorned with motifs of wild roses and leaves, ears of wheat, camellias, morning glory, and "rivers" of diamonds. Hair pins in the shape of crescent moons, stars, pine cones, or vine leaves ornamented the coiffure. The ferronnière, composed of

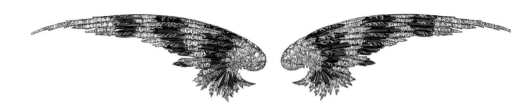

Wing Aigrette tiara created by
Joseph Chaumet for Gertrude
Vanderbilt Whitney, 1910 •
platinum, diamonds, enamel

a small chain or a strand of pearls with
a pendant at the center of the forehead,
was all the rage. The central motif could
be a pearl, a neo-Gothic motif such as
a gargoyle in oxidized silver, or a small
gold plaque with emeralds and diamonds.
Tortoiseshell combs were decorated with
reed or bouquet motifs.

Second Empire and Nineteenth Century

During the Second Empire, the tiara
was no longer the preserve of the
aristocracy; it came to symbolize the
success of the newly wealthy. At the
1855 and 1867 World's Fairs, jewelers
were still presenting collections of head
ornaments. Motifs were drawn from
antiquity, with palms, foliage, and oat
kernels, or from nature, with vine leaves,
bunches of grapes, ferns, rosebuds,
and so on. Jewelry was transformable:
a diamond-sprinkled branch of lilac,
created by Rouvenat in 1867, could be
used "either as a bodice brooch or hair
ornament." A floral tiara with diamonds
and turquoises designed by Mellerio
could be separated into eight brooches.
The aigrette, inspired by a bird's plume,
could be pinned onto a hat; in steel and
diamonds, it always sparkled.

Belle Époque

The tiara was back in fashion again,
with designs that could be transformed
into a necklace. Jewelry houses such as
Chaumet, Boucheron, and Cartier were
receiving more and more special orders.
The pieces were narrower, set with pearls
or precious stones—especially diamonds—
and featured symmetrical, Greco-Roman,
or Louis XVI motifs, or were naturalistic in
theme, with ears of wheat, daisies, or wild
roses. Among the more original designs
was one made by Chaumet in 1910 for
Gertrude Vanderbilt Whitney, composed
of a spectacular pair of diamond-encrusted

wings in platinum and enamel. Diamond aigrettes were adorned with crescent moons or bouquets of pendant drops held with a bow. Some could be worn as a brooch. Tortoiseshell hair pins, designed to hold back loose locks without flattening them, had fishnet or laurel leaf motifs in platinum set with diamonds.

Art Nouveau

Head ornaments were extremely imaginative and luxurious. Combs and tiaras drew inspiration from Japanese-style imagery of ever-changing nature, using the adularescence, or luster, of moonstone, the iridescence of opal, or the subtle shades of translucent enamels combined with patinated horn. Jewelers composed dreamlike landscapes. In *Les Modes* in 1902, Gabriel Mourey described a tiara by Fouquet that was made of "seaweed in translucent pinkish-green enamel with blisters of opal and water droplets of brilliants, from which blossoms a strange seaflower whose petals are cut from seashells, with pinkish pearls of a delightful hue."

Art Deco

After World War I, head ornaments adopted a simpler line and geometric forms. The bandeau tiara was worn low on the forehead, with motifs in platinum and gemstones. It could be transformed into a bracelet, brooch, or necklace. Aigrettes were affixed to hats. With the fashion for short hair in the 1920s, tortoiseshell combs disappeared, while wigmakers created round combs with a mass of curls to wear at the nape of the neck. Women who weren't sporting a bob would flatten and pull back their hair into a small chignon into which a large, fan-shaped comb could be inserted; these were often in carved tortoiseshell or gold lace embroidered with precious stones. In the 1930s, hair was worn longer, lightly curled or crimped, with a barrette placed near the parting or on the left side of the coiffure, while pearl pins sought "to fix wide, wavy . . . forms on short curls." Tiaras then fell into disuse. However, they continued to be worn on ceremonial occasions and at aristocratic balls in the 1950s, as they still are, albeit more rarely, today.

VAN CLEEF & ARPELS

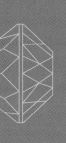

Houses, Artists, and Designers

BOUCHERO

Numerous jewelry makers and designers left their mark on the history of French jewelry between the nineteenth century and the 1950s. Their ideas gave rise to some remarkable works that are admired to this day. This selection of biographies recounts the extraordinary stories of some of the most illustrious names.

Bapst

This dynasty of Parisian jewelers was founded in Paris during the reign of Louis XV by Georges-Michel Bapst (1718–1770). His son Georges-Frédéric (1756–1826) went into partnership with Ange-Joseph Aubert, jeweler to the Crown, then with Louis-Frédéric Bachman and with Paul-Nicolas Menière, who was also jeweler to the Crown. His cousin Jacques-Evrard (or -Eberhard) joined the business and, in 1796, married Menière's daughter. The house regained its prestige under the Restoration, and Jacques-Evrard was appointed jeweler to the Crown in 1821. He created numerous jewelry pieces for the royal family. His emerald and diamond tiara for the Duchess of Angoulême—now on display at the Musée du Louvre—is a masterpiece of Restoration jewelry.

After 1830, the house took the name Bapst Frères and was headed by Jacques-Evrard's sons Paul-Constant and Charles-Eberhard. During the July Monarchy, the royal family, whose members did not wear the French Crown Jewels, commissioned jewelry privately. During the Second Empire, Paul-Alfred (1823–1879) joined the family business, which had become hugely successful. He designed numerous pieces for Empress Eugénie, which were mounted using the Crown Jewels. On Paul-Alfred's death, his son Germain Bapst (1853–1921) partnered with Lucien Falize (1838–1897), while in 1880 his cousin Jules (1830–1899) founded a new jewelry house with his son Armand and his brother Paul: J. et P. Bapst et Fils. This company carried on the family tradition until 1930.

Belperron

The designer of some exceptional jewelry pieces, Suzanne Belperron (1900–1983) imposed a style of her own: "my style is my signature," she would say—a statement that sums up well this bold avant-garde artist. After studying at the École des Beaux-Arts at Besançon, she was taken on in 1919 as a designer/model maker by Jeanne Boivin, widow of the jeweler René Boivin who had died in 1917. Belperron's arrival marked a turning point for the house, which she left in 1932, allegedly after a dispute related to her wish to add her initials to her designs. Suzanne then went into partnership with Bernard Hertz, a dealer in pearls and precious stones, to become its "exclusive, sole, and recognized artistic and technical director." At the end of World War II, following the death of Bernard Hertz in Auschwitz, she and his son, Jean Hertz, took the helm of the company, which they renamed Jean Hertz Suzanne Belperron, until its liquidation in 1974.

A woman of great talent, Suzanne Belperron designed large-sized jewelry pieces with soft, curving lines and rounded forms; she combined ornamental and precious stones with skill, playing with their translucence, transparency, and color. Her pieces were coveted by a prestigious, aristocratic, artistic, and industrial clientele, from the Duchess of Windsor to Mrs. Gary (Veronica) Cooper.

Boivin

The Boivin jewelry house, founded in 1890 by René Boivin (1864–1917), created pieces that were in keeping with the tastes of the time, mostly as special orders. On René's death, his wife, Jeanne, sister of the couturier Paul Poiret, took over the business. In 1919, she hired Suzanne Vuillerme (1900–1983)—later known as Suzanne Belperron—who would greatly contribute to the house's success with her bold, modern pieces. Originally located on Rue des Pyramides, the jeweler moved to Avenue de l'Opéra in 1931. The following year, Suzanne Belperron left Boivin.

The house had many devotees, including the writer Louise de Vilmorin, aristocrats such as the Princess de Faucigny-Lucinge, and the painter Kees van Dongen, among other prominent figures. Boivin designs were characterized at the time by their innovative designs, large size, combinations of materials, and use of colored stones. Jeanne died in 1959 and her daughter Germaine succeeded her.

Boucheron

After his apprenticeship as a jeweler, Frédéric Boucheron (1830–1902) opened a shop in 1858 under the arcades of the Palais-Royal. His nephew Georges Radius joined him in 1865. Boucheron's creativity, craftsmanship, and daring soon attracted an international clientele. He was awarded the gold medal at the 1867 World's Fair in Paris, and the grand prix at the 1889 World's Fair. In 1893, he established himself on Place Vendôme. He chose number 26, where the Comtesse de Castiglione lived on the mezzanine floor for fifteen years.

On the death of Frédéric Boucheron, his son Louis (1874–1959) took over the management of the house. A graduate of the Ponts et Chaussées engineering school in Paris, he was interested in technical discoveries such as new gem cuts. The house developed and opened subsidiaries in New York and London. It caused a sensation at the Exposition des Arts Décoratifs et Industriels Modernes in Paris in 1925. Shortly afterward, it created 149 extraordinarily beautiful jewelry pieces for the Maharaja of Patiala. In 1930, Louis Boucheron was commissioned by the Shah of Iran to value the national treasures of Persia. His sons Fred (1907–1973) and Gérard

(1910–1996) joined the company in 1932 and 1934 respectively. In the 1950s, the house enjoyed success with its experimental pieces offering a new interpretation of the plant and animal world.

Cartier

In 1847, Louis-François Cartier (1819–1904) took over the jewelry studio of Adolphe Picard. He gained a loyal clientele from both the business class and from members of the court of Napoleon III, such as Princess Mathilde.

His son Alfred (1841–1925) succeeded him in 1874 and developed an original style with the best craftsmen in the trade. His designs were inspired by the animal and plant world, but he did not adopt the art nouveau style, preferring the eighteenth-century aesthetic and the use of platinum.

Alfred's son Louis (1875–1942) went into partnership with him in 1898. The following year, the house opened premises on Rue de la Paix. Louis's brothers Pierre (1878–1964) and Jacques (1884–1941) joined the business. The house developed abroad, opening stores in London in 1902 and New York in 1909. The subsidiaries operated independently. In the early twentieth century, Cartier's garland style was popular among a high-society clientele and the aristocracy, as well as among artists.

Cartier followed technological advances and introduced decorative innovations. Under the influence of the designer Charles Jacqueau, who was hired in 1909, the house developed particular color combinations in its designs. Following Jacques Cartier's trip to India in 1911, the maharajas commissioned him to modernize their extraordinary jewels. In 1914, the panther made its appearance in the jeweler's catalogs, and went on to become an iconic symbol of the house.

At the 1925 Exposition Internationale des Arts Décoratifs et Industriels Modernes in Paris, the house opted to exhibit in the Pavillon de l'Élégance, alongside couturiers, rather than with the other jewelers at the Grand Palais.

In 1933, Jeanne Toussaint was appointed director of high jewelry. On her initiative, the Oiseau en Cage (Caged Bird) brooch was created in 1942 and became Cartier's most iconic piece at the time. After World War II, the house developed a specialty in colorful bird brooches.

Chaumet

The house of Chaumet comes from a long line of prestigious Parisian jewelers, whose origins go back to 1780. The story began with Marie-Étienne Nitot (1750–1809), who became one of the greatest jewelers of his time, under the protection of the future emperor Napoleon I. Nitot started out as a jeweler-watchmaker, established in 1780 on Rue Saint-Honoré in Paris, but his renown

CHAUMET

Place VENDOME

Nº 12

dates from Napoleon's coronation in 1804, for which Nitot made the ceremonial sword. His son François-Regnault (1779–1853) was also appointed jeweler to the emperor and empress, and, later, to the king and queen; he located the house for the first time on Place Vendôme in 1812, but withdrew on the fall of the empire in 1815.

Jean-Baptiste Fossin (1786–1848) and his son Jules (1808–1869) took over from him. They became the most fashionable jewelers of the Restoration and July Monarchy. Having no heir, Jules Fossin sold the house to his studio director, Prosper Morel (1825–1908), in 1861. After his marriage to Morel's daughter Marie, Joseph Chaumet (1852–1928) joined his father-in-law's company, taking the helm in 1889. His talent attracted an aristocratic clientele. In 1900, the house was awarded a gold medal at the World's Fair in Paris and established itself permanently on Place Vendôme in 1907.

From the early nineteenth century through the 1920s, the house was famed for its tiara designs. In 1920, Joseph Chaumet developed a process for distinguishing natural and synthetic stones. The jeweler took part in the 1925 Exposition Internationale des Arts Décoratifs et Industriels Modernes in Paris. The house's designs were highly influenced by art deco at the time.

Joseph's son Marcel Chaumet (1886–1964) succeeded him in 1928. After World War II, Marcel's sons Jacques and Pierre took the reins.

Després

Jean Després (1889–1980) was one of the most innovative designers of the interwar period. Born into a family of glassmakers, he apprenticed as a goldsmith while also taking drawing classes. He frequented the Bateau-Lavoir artists' residence in Paris, where he met Braque and Modigliani. During World War I, he became an engine draftsman for military aviation, an experience that would influence his work. After the war, he took over the family store in Avallon in Burgundy, and set up his own studio there. He earned a reputation for his modern designs, such as his Bijoux Moteurs (Engine Jewelry). His avant-garde approach was expressed through his striking designs and chosen themes, as well as in the materials he used, combining onyx, coral, and turquoise with silver.

In the 1930s, he presented his Bijoux Glaces (Mirror Jewelry), created in collaboration with Étienne Cournault (1891–1948). These surrealist-inspired works in silver with gold inserts were sometimes enameled. He had a celebrity clientele, including Josephine Baker and Jacques Doucet, and his success enabled him to establish himself in Paris, although he kept his studio in Avallon. The house continued its production until the late 1970s, with a focus on tableware in gold and silver.

"Chaumet, Place Vendôme No. 12," 1920. Preparatory sketch for an advertisement, featuring tiaras and diadems worn "*à la Joséphine*" • charcoal, gouache, and India ink on tracing paper

◆ **Dusausoy**

   This house evolved under the direction of Justin Dusausoy (1876–1960), who opened premises at 41 Boulevard des Capucines in Paris in 1912. It initially specialized in buying and selling antique jewelry and hardstones, and it was the customization of antique pieces that led the house to produce modern jewelry.

   In 1925, Dusausoy took part in the Exposition Internationale des Arts Décoratifs et Industriels Modernes, where it was awarded a grand prix for its original designs, which included the Stalactite bracelet. After Madrid in 1927 and Athens and Rotterdam in 1928, the house presented jewelry the following year at the Musée Galliera, in Paris, at the exhibition *Les arts de la bijouterie, joaillerie, orfèvrerie.* One of the designs on display was a ring with a diamond-encrusted ball set on three circular tiers and flanked with two stepped motifs. It was designs such as these that led to Dusausoy being as famous a name as Cartier and Boucheron in the 1930s. The house closed in the 1970s.

◆ **Falize**

   The house of Falize encompassed three generations of jewelers. In 1833, Alexis Falize (1811–1898) worked for "M. Mellerio known as Meller" as an administrative clerk, and his curiosity for the trade and his drawing skills caught his employer's attention. His talent was put to good use: he began by finishing off the design sketches, then went on to design parures himself. In 1835, he was hired by Janisset. He set up his own business in 1838, after buying Aristide Joureau-Robin's studios at the Palais-Royal and agreeing to work exclusively for Janisset.

   The Janisset house did not survive the Revolution of 1848, but Falize was approached by numerous jewelers. From the 1860s, he was famed for his use of cloisonné enamel, inspired by the arts of the Far East, Persia, China, and especially Japan. His collaboration with the enamel artist Antoine Tard marked a turning point. In 1869, the Union Centrale des Arts Décoratifs invited him to exhibit alongside Japanese artists. A recognized figure of the trade, Falize was president of the Chambre Syndicale des Bijoutiers et Joailliers from 1864 to 1874. In 1876, he passed the reins of his business over to his son Lucien.

   Lucien (1839–1897) had worked with his father since 1856, going into partnership with him in 1871 and developing the reputation of the house. Like his father, he had a passion for Japanese art and was inspired by its plant and animal imagery. The father and son's close collaboration until 1876 makes it hard to determine which of them designed the famous cloisonné enamels on gold foil. In 1878, Lucien participated in the World's Fair in Paris and was awarded the Légion d'Honneur, as well as one of the three grands prix. His designs were in various styles: neo-Gothic and neo-Renaissance, Indian, and Japanese.

In 1880, Lucien partnered with Germain Bapst, a descendant of the famous family of jewelers to the Crown, and they participated in the 1889 World's Fair. In the same period, Lucien—a great and erudite connoisseur of the history of jewelry and an active member of the Union Centrale des Arts Décoratifs—wrote extensive exhibition reviews and articles for arts magazines. His son André (1872–1936) took over the house with his brothers, Jean (1874–1943) and Pierre (1875–1953), under the name Falize Frères. The house won two grands prix at the 1900 World's Fair. Pierre—a painter and sculptor—soon parted ways with his brothers, and Jean withdrew from the business at the end of World War I. In 1930, the company encountered financial difficulties and closed on the death of André Falize in 1936.

Fontenay

Eugène Fontenay (1823–1887), the son and grandson of jewelers, expressed his desire to continue the family tradition early on. He was an apprentice to Édouard Marchand and at the Dutreih jewelry house, before setting up his business in 1847. For the 1855 World's Fair, he created a tiara "of extreme delicacy," as described by Vever, which was naturalistic in inspiration and decorated with a branch of wild bramble with its fruits and flowers. Three years later, he created a tiara with fleurons for Empress Eugénie that could be arranged in four different ways, depending on the choice of gems. Fontenay went into partnership with Joseph Halphen, one of the leading dealers in precious stones, with ties to the Far East and Egypt. His passion for classical jewelry was showcased at the 1867 World's Fair, with designs of Greek and Etruscan inspiration. After the destruction of the Summer Palace of the Emperor of China, he would use jadeite for amphora-shaped earrings and insect-shaped brooches. In 1869, the year the Suez Canal was completed, he presented neo-Egyptian jewelry.

Fontenay was appointed a member of the jury for the 1873 and 1878 World's Fairs. In 1882, he handed over his business to his principal collaborator, Henri Smets, and devoted himself to writing. He was one of the first to record the history of jewelry in his book *Les Bijoux anciens et modernes*, published posthumously in 1887.

Fouquet

Three generations of jewelers developed the house of Fouquet. Alphonse Fouquet (1828–1911) started the dynasty. At the age of eleven, he began his apprenticeship, working for various jewelers, notably Alexis Falize and Léon Rouvenat. In 1860, he went into partnership with Eugène Deshayes. Their collaboration lasted only two years, but it launched the house of Fouquet, which soon numbered over thirty workers and exported its production throughout Europe and to South America. At the 1878 World's Fair, Fouquet presented several jewelry pieces inspired by antiquity and, in particular, the Renaissance, featuring painted enamels by Béranger and Paul Grandhomme. In 1883, some of the pieces he presented at the Amsterdam International Colonial and Export Exhibition caused a stir: the use of the female figure in designs for women was considered highly unorthodox by some.

In 1891, Alphonse was joined by his son Georges (1862–1957), who succeeded him in 1895. Georges broke with his father's style and inspirations by working with the designer Charles Desrosiers. Now, the house's designs were inspired by nature, the main theme of the art nouveau style. For the 1900 World's Fair, Fouquet worked with the Czech artist Alphonse Mucha (1860–1939). From 1909, Fouquet's jewelry moved toward more pared-down forms and incorporated the use of platinum.

Jean Fouquet (1899–1984) worked with his father from 1919, producing strict, highly geometric designs in silver, white gold, and platinum, then polished or chrome-plated steel. These metals were combined with lacquer and sometimes large colored gemstones, or smaller, graduated stones. A member of the Union des Artistes Modernes and the Association des Étudiants et des Artistes Révolutionnaires, Jean continued to create and exhibit work until 1960, following the closure of the house of Fouquet in 1936.

Froment-Meurice

The son of the Parisian goldsmith Jean-Joseph Froment, known as Jean-François (1773–1803), François-Désiré (1801–1855) lost his father at a very young age. His mother remarried, to the goldsmith Pierre-Jacques Meurice (1781–1857). The family business was passed on to François-Désiré, who added his stepfather's name to his own in the 1830s. At his first presentation of gold- and silverwork and jewelry at the Exposition des Produits de l'Industrie in 1839, he was awarded a double silver medal, with gold medals following at the same event in 1844 and 1849. Claude-Philibert Rambuteau, the Préfet of Paris and the Seine, reintroduced for his benefit the honorary title of goldsmith-jeweler of the City of Paris, which had been abolished in 1793. The Great Exhibition in London in 1851 was also a huge success: Froment-Meurice won the prestigious Council Medal. But this meteoric rise came to an abrupt end with his death, a few months before the 1855 World's Fair, where he would be awarded a posthumous honorary medal.

Froment-Meurice's success stemmed from his ability to translate the romantic sensibility of his time through his choice of subjects, inspired by the chivalric and Christian themes of the

(From top to bottom) Left: Dusausoy pendant, Aucoc brooch; center: Chaumet necklace, Georges Fouquet brooch; right: Sandoz pendant, Mauboussin brooch; bottom: Georges Fouquet bracelet, from *L'Illustration*, December 3, 1927

Middle Ages. His jewelry designs in oxidized and enameled silver would shift toward a naturalistic, enameled gold neo-Renaissance iconography. Froment-Meurice managed to surround himself with great artists, as Théophile Gautier commented in 1855: "Like the conductor of an orchestra, he inspired and led a whole world of sculptors, designers, ornamentists, engravers, enamelers, and jewelers." His clientele was made up of aristocrats as well as writers, including Honoré de Balzac and Victor Hugo.

His son Émile (1837–1913) took the helm in 1859 until 1907. He continued the family tradition, drawing inspiration from the Renaissance in particular. He successfully participated in the 1867, 1878, and 1889 World's Fairs, and at the 1900 fair he was awarded a grand prix for his gold- and silverwork.

Lacloche

While the name Lacloche was recorded in 1808 close to Maastricht—a city annexed by France at the time—the history of this jewelry house began in Belgium, with four brothers. In 1892, Léopold (1863–1921) and Jules (1867–1937) Lacloche left Brussels and established themselves as jewelers in Paris, setting up a partnership. Six years later, they joined forces with the jeweler Gompers.

In the same period, the other two Lacloche brothers, Fernand (1868–1932) and Jacques (1865–1900), set up business in Madrid, in 1895, where they attracted a prestigious clientele. After the death of Jacques in 1900, Fernand joined his two elder brothers in Paris, where Lacloche opened premises at 15 Rue de la Paix as well as a branch in London.

The house won acclaim at the Exposition Internationale des Arts Décoratifs et Industriels Modernes in 1925, particularly for its jewelry inspired by the *Fables* of La Fontaine, and was awarded a grand prix. The main characteristics of art deco jewelry design were reflected in their elegant pieces, and the company became very successful. Lacloche participated in the *Arts de la bijouterie, joaillerie, orfèvrerie* exhibition at the Musée Galliera in Paris in 1929. In 1931, the company was declared bankrupt, but Jacques Lacloche (1901–1999), son of Jacques, relaunched the name. In 1936, he rented a showcase at the Carlton hotel in Cannes, then in 1938 opened a store on Place Vendôme. He abandoned jewelry production in the 1960s.

Lalique

René Lalique (1860–1945) began his apprenticeship at the age of sixteen with the Aucoc jewelry house, while pursuing his studies at the École des Arts Décoratifs. Two years later, he left to study art in England, as the art schools there were more avant-garde at the time. In 1882, Lalique became an independent designer for a number of jewelry houses, producing works that already had a characteristic lightness. In 1885, he bought the studio of the jeweler Jules Destapes on Place Gaillon in Paris and worked for the important Paris jewelry houses. His success led him to acquire a new studio, before moving all of his business activities to 20 Rue Thérèse, on the corner of Avenue de l'Opéra. René Lalique made spectacularly large costume jewelry for the actress Sarah Bernhardt, while Calouste Gulbenkian—a businessman and great collector of objets d'art—gave him carte blanche to design a set of jewelry for him.

In 1893, René Lalique began to exhibit at various art fairs and other events. His jewelry designs heralded the emergence of a new style. After his highly successful participation at the 1900 World's Fair in Paris, he became one of the great figures of art nouveau. Lalique drew inspiration from nature and made innovative use of materials that had fallen out of favor, such as glass, enamel, and mother-of-pearl. He often preferred hardstones or ornamental stones to precious stones. He received commissions from all over the world, and took part in all the major fairs and exhibitions of his time, in France and abroad (such as Turin in 1902 and Saint Louis, Missouri, in 1904).

In 1905, Lalique opened a store on Place Vendôme, where he presented both his jewelry and his objects made of glass. He became increasingly interested in glass design and production, with his last jewelry exhibition taking place in 1912. Afterward, he became a full-time master glassmaker. In 1933, all of his work was exhibited at the Musée des Arts Décoratifs in Paris. On his death, his son Marc succeeded him at the helm of the Wingen-sur-Moder factory in Alsace.

Mauboussin

The story of Mauboussin began in 1827 with the opening of a jewelry store by a certain M. Rocher. His collaborator, Jean-Baptiste Noury, took over the business. Having acquired a good reputation, Noury took part in the Vienna World's Fair of 1873 and the Paris World's Fair of 1878, where he was awarded a bronze medal.

Noury's nephew Georges Mauboussin (1862–1954), who apprenticed at the house, bought out the business in 1898. With his designs that were typical of the contemporary art deco style, he participated in most of the significant events of the time, including the Exposition Internationale des Arts Décoratifs et Industriels Modernes in 1925. In 1928, subsidiaries were opened in New York, London, and Buenos Aires.

From 1928 to 1931, the house held themed exhibitions on the emerald, ruby, and diamond, which boosted its renown, notably with regard to gemstones. Its clientele included royalty, such as the

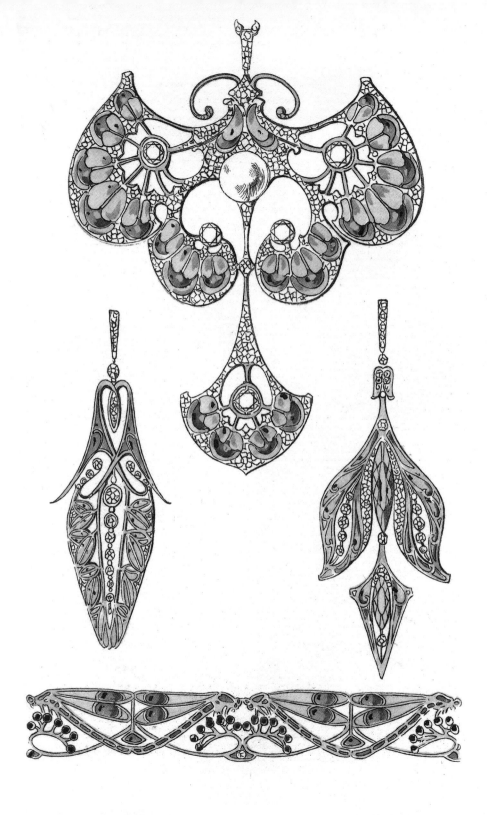

Maharaja of Indore, as well as the actresses Marlene Dietrich and Greta Garbo.

Pierre Mauboussin (1900–1984) left his mark on the house with his inventiveness and pared-down style, before devoting himself to the study of aerodynamics. After World War II, the house acquired its address at 20 Place Vendôme, thereby joining the ranks of other great jewelry houses, such as Boucheron, Chaumet, and Van Cleef & Arpels.

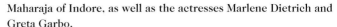 Mellerio

Members of the Mellerio family first arrived in France from Italy in the sixteenth century, but it was in the late eighteenth and early nineteenth centuries that the jewelry house of the same name was established.

Jean-Baptiste Mellerio (1765–1850) opened his shop À la Couronne de Fer (The Iron Crown) on Rue Vivienne in Paris. The house's position strengthened during the First Empire. François Mellerio (1772–1843) had many prestigious clients, including Empress Joséphine, Pauline Bonaparte (one of Napoleon's sisters), and several field marshals. In 1815, the house was located on Rue de la Paix, very close to Place Vendôme. Mellerio's success continued during the Restoration, notably thanks to the royal family.

The French economy slowed considerably as a result of the Revolution of 1848, prompting Jean-François Mellerio (1815–1886) and his brother Antoine (1816–1882) to open a subsidiary in Madrid.

The Second Empire brought an unprecedented period of prosperity for the house. The store on Rue de la Paix was visited by the most famous figures of the time, and Empress Eugénie made numerous purchases. Antoine Mellerio played an active role in the founding of the Chambre Syndicale de la Bijouterie, Joaillerie, Orfèvrerie. The house exhibited pieces at the Paris World's Fairs, winning a medal of honor in 1855 and a gold medal in 1878. Throughout the twentieth century, the house adapted its designs to follow the major artistic styles. Descendants of the Mellerio family are still in charge of the house today.

Sterlé

On the death of his father during World War I, Pierre Sterlé (1905–1978) was entrusted to the care of an uncle, who was a jeweler. Sterlé began his career working for the jewelry houses Chaumet and Boucheron, among others. In 1934, he opened a studio on Rue Sainte-Anne in Paris, then in 1945 he moved his business activities to Avenue de l'Opéra, close to Place Vendôme. The writer Colette was one of his first clients and, later, he garnered an international clientele, notably the Maharani of

Baroda. Renowned in the 1940s and 1950s for his creative originality and technical expertise, Sterlé was very much inspired by nature, and he used many different gemstones and unusual materials such as seashell. His brooches became his signature pieces. At the end of his career, he developed close ties with Chaumet, which bought his stock in 1976.

◈ Templier

Charles Templier (1821–1884) founded his jewelry house in 1849. His son Paul (1860–1948) took over after his death. In the early twentieth century, Paul Templier took part in the major exhibitions of the time and was awarded several grands prix and medals. In 1911, his son Raymond Templier (1891–1968) participated in the Salon de la Société des Artistes Décorateurs and went on to become one of the great art deco jewelers. At the 1925 Exposition Internationale des Arts Décoratifs et Industriels Modernes, he won acclaim for his geometric jewelry pieces. The actresses Brigitte Helm and Marie Glory wore his designs in Marcel L'Herbier's 1928 film *L'Argent*.

A founding member of the Union des Artistes Modernes in 1929, Raymond Templier was appointed secretary to the management committee, and he formed part of the circle of avant-garde artists who transformed the history of the decorative arts. In 1937, the Templier house participated in the Exposition Internationale des Arts et des Techniques Appliqués à la Vie Moderne.

In 1954, the journal *Mobilier et Décoration* devoted an article to the jeweler: "Raymond Templier, architecte du bijou" (Raymond Templier: Architect of jewelry). A sportsman, Templier also designed trophies and posters for numerous sporting events.

◈ Van Cleef & Arpels

This jewelry house was founded in 1906 when Alfred Van Cleef (1872–1938) went into partnership with his wife's brothers, who successively joined the business. The company was located next to Lalique, at 22 Place Vendôme, which remains the jeweler's iconic address to this day. Branches opened elsewhere in France, mostly at fashionable coastal resorts. The house took part in the Exposition Internationale des Arts Décoratifs et Industriels Modernes in 1925 and won a grand prix for its Roses bracelet made of emeralds, rubies, and diamonds.

In 1926, the founding couple's daughter, Renée Puissant, became artistic director, in collaboration with the designer René-Sim Lacaze. Together, they cultivated the creativity of the house, launching the Serti Mystérieux setting in 1933, in which specially grooved, square-cut stones were inserted in such a way as to render the setting completely invisible. In 1934, the house produced the Ludo bracelet with its clasp that resembled a jeweled belt buckle. The Passe-Partout was created in 1938—a piece that could be transformed into a necklace, dress clip, or bracelet.

At the outbreak of World War II, most of the Arpels family emigrated to the United States. The house established itself in New York in 1939, opening a store at 744 Fifth Avenue in 1942. The first Inséparables clips depicting couples or birds were created two years later.

In 1950, a masterpiece of inventiveness was born: the Zip necklace, which could be worn as a necklace or zipped up to form a bracelet. In 1954, Van Cleef & Arpels became the first jewelry house on Place Vendôme to offer more affordable pieces, such as the Lion Ébouriffé (Tousled Lion) and the Chat Malicieux (Mischievous Cat). It continues to develop its business today.

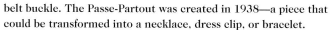 Vever

Pierre-Paul Vever (c. 1795–1853) opened a jewelry shop in Metz in 1821. His son Jean-Jacques Ernest (1823–1884) trained as a jeweler and went on to complete his studies in Germany and Austria. In 1848, he took the reins from his father. He presented several pieces at the 1861 World's Fair in Metz.

The Vever family established itself in Paris after the Franco-Prussian war in 1870, when Ernest took over the business of Gustave Baugrand, who died during the Siege of Paris. In 1875, he became the president of the Chambre Syndicale de la Bijouterie, Joaillerie, Orfèvrerie. Appointed a member of the jury at the 1878 World's Fair, he presented his designs—including an Assyrian-style choker in chased gold—as a non-competing participant. His sons Paul (1851–1915) and Henri (1854–1942) succeeded him in 1881, with Paul managing the house while Henri oversaw the artistic side of the business.

At the 1889 World's Fair, Vever won one of the grands prix for jewelry. Its designs were already largely inspired by the plant and animal world, and the trend continued until the 1900 World's Fair; the house was one of the champions of the art nouveau style and was awarded a grand prix for its creations as a whole at the fair. One of the jeweler's characteristic designs was the Sylvia pendant, in the form of a winged creature—half woman, half butterfly—in agate, with a bodice of rubies and diamonds, and translucent wings, gown, and train in enamel.

In the same period, from 1906 to 1908, Henri Vever published a three-volume reference book, *La Bijouterie française au XIX*[e] *siècle: 1800–1900*, tracing the history of jewelry. In 1924, he donated his collection of nineteenth-century French jewelry to the Musée des Arts Décoratifs in Paris. Paul's sons André and Pierre headed the house from 1921 to 1960.

Practical
Advice:
Appraisal and Valuation,
Buying, Selling, Insurance

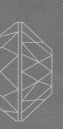

Appraisal and Valuation

Before parting with an antique jewelry piece, it is advisable to have it professionally appraised to obtain confirmation of its value. Moreover, in the case of theft, the insurer must be provided with proof of the item's worth. Only an expert appraisal enables jewelry to be insured at its correct value in order to receive proper compensation. An appraisal is also required for the administration of an estate, to determine assets as precisely as possible and to share them among family members objectively and equitably.

The assessment and valuation of antique jewelry is complex and requires specialist knowledge and skills, so it is preferable to consult a connoisseur affiliated with a professional body or a recognized association of experts. The appraisal must always be written and include at least the following elements, for each item: the nature of the material, a description of the piece, the period, the gemstones, and condition of the item, with one or more accompanying photos. These documents should ideally be kept in a secure place such as a bank vault.

Buying and Selling

A professional will always issue a purchase receipt (or bill of sale in the case of an auctioneer), specifying the nature, composition, origin, and period of the piece. For jewelry ornamented with gemstones, the gemological laboratory certificate may be included.

Secondhand and antique dealers
These dealers sell their goods at their stores or at events such as flea markets and antique fairs, where private individuals and collectors can purchase interesting jewelry items at reasonable prices. This is also a quick and easy way to sell one's jewelry, because payment is received immediately. It is advisable to get several opinions before accepting an offer. Jewelry can also be left with a consignment store, in which case the seller or dealer will only receive a commission, but it may take a long time to sell the item.

Jewelry specialists
Such specialists may be antique dealers, professional art dealers, or jewelers who sell antique or secondhand jewelry. They have extensive knowledge of the field and are among the best placed to evaluate a finely made piece of jewelry. Most of these professionals are members of trade associations or professional bodies and must respect specific codes of conduct. Consignment with a specialist dealer is also possible.

Auction houses
An auctioneer organizes regular public sales of jewelry. A pre-auction viewing enables potential buyers to inspect the

jewelry in the sale, and an expert who can provide specific information may be on hand. In the absence of a viewing, it is usually possible to consult a sales catalog or the auction house's website. One should be wary of photographs, however, which may be deceptively flattering. The potential buyer must also be aware of the conditions of sale, which can vary from one auction house to another. They are generally on display.

During the sale, a gesture to the auctioneer indicates a bid, which is a commitment to buy. It is advisable to set a maximum purchase price before the start of the sale. It is possible to place a maximum bid in advance, or to bid live by telephone or online. The auction house's fees and charges are added to the hammer price.

In the case of the sale of an item of jewelry, an appointment is made with the auctioneer, who provides an initial valuation. A contract is then signed, indicating the identity of the seller, the type of sale, and the reserve price (if applicable), as well as the fees, charges, and taxes payable by the seller. Prior

to the sale, the jewelry is stored by the auctioneer. There may be a long wait before it is auctioned: a sale devoted to jewelry, with a dedicated catalog, is preferable to a general sale. It is also best for an expert to be present. There is no guarantee that the consignment will find a buyer and if an item does not reach its reserve price, it can be withdrawn. Once the sale has taken place, it may take one or two months to receive the payment.

In France, auction sales—most of which are devoted to jewelry and watches—are also held by the Crédit Municipale: a public institution whose activity is based on the principle of pawnbroking. After valuation, an advance in the form of a collateral loan is paid to the owner. The item is sold within a legal period of three months. The difference between the sale price and the amount of the loan is paid on average two weeks after the sale, less the fees and interest due.

Insurance

Items of jewelry are among the assets most liable to theft. Several types of insurance provide protection against this risk, and others, such as damage or loss. Standard homeowners insurance generally covers jewelry that is stolen or destroyed in a fire; however, it doesn't usually cover lost items, and the payout limit could be below the value of the jewelry. Additional coverage or a contract with a stand-alone jewelry insurer may be advisable.

In the case of theft, the compensation is calculated according to the jewelry's market value, within the limits of the sum insured. Insurers generally base their calculation on the average selling prices at public auction, including fees, or on the prices charged by antique jewelry dealers. The owner must provide supporting documents (receipts, appraisals), photographs, and sometimes proof of enhanced home security measures.

Bibliography

M any publications (books, exhibition catalogs, history reference works, biographies, and articles) were consulted in the preparation of this book. The following works will enable readers to find out more about the subject.

 Jewelry through Time

BABELON, Ernst. *La Gravure en pierres fines: Camées et intailles*. Paris: Librairies-Imprimeries Réunies, 1894.

BAPST, Germain. *Histoire des joyaux de la couronne de France*. Paris: Hachette, 1889.

BAYARD, Émile. *L'Art de reconnaître les bijoux anciens, pierres précieuses, métal précieux*. Paris: Gründ, 1924.

BAYER, Patricia, et al. *Jewelry Design Source Book*. New York: Van Nostrand Reinhold Company, 1989.

BECKER, Vivienne. *Art Nouveau Jewelry*. London: Thames & Hudson, 1998.

BENNETT, David, and Daniela MASCETTI. *Célébration du bijou: Bijoux exceptionnels des XIXe et XXe siècles*. Paris: La Bibliothèque des Arts, 2012.

BLACK, J. Anderson. *The Story of Jewelry*. New York: William Morrow, 1974.

BLANCHOT, I.-L. *Les Bijoux anciens*. Paris: Les Éditions Pittoresques, 1929.

CAILLES, Françoise. *Bijoux anciens*. Paris: Duncan/Actes Sud, 1997.

———. *Bijoux de l'Antiquité à nos jours*. Paris: Argus Valentine's, 2005.

CAPPELLIERI, Alba. *Twentieth-Century Jewellery: From Art Nouveau to Contemporary Design in Europe and the United States*. Milan: Skira, 2010.

DE CERVAL, Marguerite, ed. *Dictionnaire international du bijou*. Paris: Éditions du Regard, 1998.

DEWIEL, Lydia L. *Les Bijoux du classicisme à l'Art déco*. Paris: Duculot, 1980.

DIDEROT, Denis. *Le Rond d'Alembert, Jean Encyclopédie ou Dictionnaire raisonné des sciences, des arts et des métiers*. Paris, c. 1762.

FONTENAY, Eugène. *Les Bijoux anciens et modernes*. Paris: Maison Quantin, 1887.

FRÉGNAC, Claude. *Les Bijoux de la Renaissance à la Belle Époque*. Paris: Hachette, 1966.

FULLÉE, Caroline. *Bijoux du XXe siècle*. Paris: Celiv, 1992.

GABARDI, Melissa, ed. *Les Bijoux: De l'Art déco aux années 40*. Paris: Les Éditions de l'Amateur, 1986.

———. *Les Bijoux des années 50*. Paris: Les Éditions de l'Amateur, 1987.

GREGORIETTI, Guido. *Jewelry through the Ages*. London: Paul Hamlyn, 1969.

HEINIGER, Jean, and Ernst ALBRECHT. *The Great Book of Jewels*. Boston: New York Graphic Society, 1974.

Hue-Williams, Sarah. *Christie's Guide to Jewellery.* Paris: Assouline, 2001.

Hughes, Graham. *The Art of Jewelry.* London: Peerage, 1972.

Joannis, Claudette. *Bijoux des régions de France.* Paris: Flammarion, 1992.

Lanllier, Jean, and Marie-Anne Pini. *Cinq siècles de joaillerie en Occident.* Paris: La Bibliothèque des Arts, 1971.

Larousse. *Joyaux et pierres précieuses.* Paris: Larousse, 2017.

Lejard, André, ed. *L'Orfèvrerie, la Joaillerie.* Paris: Éditions du Chêne, 1942.

Lenfant, Jacques. *Bijouterie-joaillerie.* Paris: Dessain et Tolra/Chêne, 1979.

Malaguzzi, Silvia. *Bijoux, pierres et objets précieux.* Paris: Hazan, 2008.

Martin, Étienne. *Bijoux Art nouveau: Nancy 1890–1920.* Strasbourg: Éditions du Quotidien, 2015.

Meylan, Vincent. *Bijoux de reines.* Paris: Assouline, 2002.

Morel, Bernard. *Les Joyaux de la couronne de France.* Antwerp/Paris: Fonds Mercator/Albin Michel, 1988.

Neret, Gilles. *Ces bijoux qui font rêver.* Paris: Solar, 1990.

Perret, Vivianne. *Mille et un carats: Joyaux, perles et autres pierreries qui ont fait l'Histoire.* Paris: La Librairie Vuibert, 2012.

Possémé, Évelyne. *Bijouterie joaillerie.* Paris: Massin, 1995.

———, and Dominique Forest. *La Collection de bijoux du musée des Arts décoratifs à Paris.* Paris: Union Centrale des Arts Décoratifs, 2004.

Raulet, Sylvie. *Bijoux Art déco.* Paris: Éditions du Regard, 1991.

———. *Bijoux des années 1940-1950.* Paris: Éditions du Regard, 1987.

Roger-Miles, Léon. *La Bijouterie.* Paris: Hachette, 1895.

Scarisbrick, Diana, et al. *Joaillerie: "Le livre."* London: Florilège, 1990.

Scordia, Lydwine. *Le Goût des bijoux du Moyen Âge aux années Art déco.* Paris: Perrin, 2013.

van Strydonck de Burkel, Rolende. *Le Bijou Art nouveau en Europe.* Paris: La Bibliothèque des Arts, 1998.

Vever, Henri. *La Bijouterie française au xixe siècle 1800-1900.* Paris: Floury, 1906–1908, 3 vols., I Consulat Empire Restauration Louis-Philippe, 1906; II Le second Empire, 1908; III La IIIe République, 1908.

Viruega, Jacqueline. *La Bijouterie parisienne 1860-1914: Du second Empire à la Première Guerre mondiale.* Paris: L'Harmattan, 2004.

Ward, Anne, John Cherry, Charlotte Gere, and Barbara Cartlidge. *Rings Through the Ages.* New York: Rizzoli, 1981.

Exhibition catalogs

Grand Palais. *Des Grands Moghols aux maharajahs: Joyaux de la collection Al Thani.* Paris: Réunion des Musées Nationaux, 2016.

Hôtel Solvay. *Le Bijou 1900.* Brussels: Les Ateliers d'Art Graphique Meddens, 1965.

Musée des Arts Décoratifs. *Bijoux Art déco et avant-garde.* Paris: Les Arts Décoratifs/Norma, 2009.

Musée du Louvre. *Dix siècles de joaillerie française.* Paris: Ministère d'État Affaires Culturelles, 1962.

Musée National de Malmaison. *Bijoux des deux Empires: Mode et sentiment 1804-1870.* Paris: Somogy, 2004.

Musée de la Vie Bourguignonne Perrin de Puycousin. *Pense à moi.* Dijon: Musée de la Vie Bourguignonne Perrin de Puycousin, 1992.

Musée de la Vie Romantique. *Bijoux romantiques 1820-1850: La parure à l'époque de George Sand.* Paris: Paris-Musées, 2000.

Materials

ARMINJON, Catherine, James BEAUPUIS, and Michèle BILIMOFF. *Dictionnaire des poinçons de fabricants d'ouvrages d'or et d'argent de Paris et de la Seine, 1798-1838.* Vols. 1 and 2. Paris: Imprimerie Nationale, 1991, 1994.

BEUQUE, Émile. *Platine, or et argent: Dictionnaire des poinçons officiels français et étrangers, anciens et modernes, de leur création (XIVe siècle) à nos jours.* Vols. 1 and 2. Paris: F. de Nobele, 1962.

BEUQUE, Émile, and Marcel FRAPSAUCE. *Dictionnaire des poinçons de maîtres orfèvres français du XIVe siècle à 1838.* Paris: F. de Nobele, 1964.

CHALABI, Maryannick, and Marie-Reine JAZÉ-CHARVOLIN. *Poinçons des fabricants d'or et d'argent, Lyon 1798-1940.* Paris: Imprimerie Nationale, 1993.

CHANLOT, Andrée. *Les Ouvrages en cheveux: Leurs secrets.* Paris: self-published, 1986.

MARFOUNINE, A. S. *L'Or.* Paris: G. Lachurié, 1988.

MARKEZANA, Yves. *Les Poinçons français d'or, d'argent, de platine de 1275 à nos jours.* Paris: Vial, 2005.

 Gemstones

ASSOCIATION FRANÇAISE DE GEMMOLOGIE. *Gemmes de l'AFG,* 4th edition. Paris: Association Française de Gemmologie, 2020.

BARBOT, Charles. *Guide pratique du joaillier ou traité complet des pierres précieuses: Leur étude chimique et minéralogique.* Paris: J. Hetzel et Cie, c. 1860.

BARIAND, Pierre, and Jean-Paul POIROT. *Larousse des pierres précieuses.* Paris: Larousse, 2004.

BOULLIARD, Jean-Claude, ed. *Pierres précieuses: Guide pratique d'identification.* Paris: Publibook, 2015.

CAILLES, Françoise. *Merveilleuses perles: Répertoire raisonné des pierres célèbres.* Paris: Argus Valentine's, 2006.

FARGES, François. *À la découverte des minéraux et pierres précieuses: Minéraux et gemmes, sachez les reconnaître.* Paris: Dunod, 2018.

MALAGUZZI, Silvia. *The Pearl.* New York: Rizzoli, 2001.

MEYLAN, Vincent. *Un siècle d'émeraudes.* Paris: VM Publications, 2020.

RAMBOSSON, Jean. *Les Pierres précieuses et les principaux ornements.* Paris: Librairie de Firmin Didot frères, fils et Cie, 1870.

RAULET, Sylvie. *Cristal de roche.* Paris: Assouline, 1999

SCHUMANN, Walter. *Gemstones of the World.* New York and London: Sterling, 2009.

DE TUGNY, Anne. *Guide des pierres de rêve.* Paris: Flammarion, 1987.

Exhibition catalogs
Le Diamant. Paris: G. Mauboussin, 1931.
Marchands de perles: Redécouverte d'une saga commerciale entre le Golfe et la France à l'aube du XXe siècle. Paris: l'École des Arts Joailliers, with the support of Van Cleef & Arpels, 2019.

Rubis, lumière de joie. Paris: G. Mauboussin, 1928.

MUSÉUM NATIONAL D'HISTOIRE NATURELLE. *Diamants: Au cœur de la Terre, au cœur des étoiles, au cœur du pouvoir.* Paris: Gallimard, 2001.

MUSÉUM NATIONAL D'HISTOIRE NATURELLE. *Gems.* Translated by Alexandra Keens. Paris: Flammarion, 2020.

 ## Main Types of Jewelry

FEDER, Soraya. *Le Collier.* Paris: Parangon, 2000.

LAMBERT, Sylvie. *La Bague: Parcours historique et symbolique.* Paris: Éditions du Collectionneur, 1998.

LENFANT, Jacques. *Le Livre de la chaîne.* Lausanne: Scriptar, 1996.

MASCETTI, Daniela, and Amanda TRIOSSI. *Earrings: From Antiquity to the Present.* New York: Rizzoli, 1990.

POSSÉMÉ, Évelyne. *Épingles de cravate.* Paris: Réunion des Musées Nationaux, 1992.

SCARISBRICK, Diana. *Portrait Jewels: Opulence and Intimacy from the Medici to the Romanovs.* New York: Thames & Hudson, 2011.

———. *Rings: Jewelry of Power, Love and Loyalty.* London: Thames & Hudson, 2007.

———. *Rings: Symbols of Wealth, Power and Affection.* New York: Harry N. Abrams, 1993.

———. *Timeless Tiaras: Chaumet from 1804 to the Present.* New York: Assouline, 2002.

Exhibition catalogs

ABBAYE DE DAOULAS. *Couronnes du monde.* Briec: Abbaye de Daoulas, 1989.

L'ÉCOLE DES ARTS JOAILLIERS. *Bagues d'hommes.* Paris: l'École des Arts Joailliers, with the support of Van Cleef & Arpels, 2018.

L'ÉCOLE DES ARTS JOAILLIERS. *Paradis d'oiseaux.* Paris: l'École des Arts Joailliers, with the support of Van Cleef & Arpels, 2019.

MUSÉE DE LA CHEMISERIE ET DE L'ÉLÉGANCE MASCULINE. *Bijoux d'hommes: Signes et insignes.* Argenton-sur-Creuse: Musée de la Chemiserie et de l'Élégance masculine, 1999.

 ## Houses, Artists, and Designers

DE CERVAL, Marguerite. *Mauboussin.* Paris: Éditions du Regard, 1992.

CHAILLE, François, and Éric NUSSBAUM. *The Cartier Collection: Jewelry.* Paris: Flammarion, 2004.

CHAUMET. *Une pléiade de maîtres joailliers 1780–1930.* Paris: J. Chaumet, 1930.

CLAIS, Anne-Marie. *Van Cleef & Arpels.* Paris: Assouline, 2001.

GABARDI, Mélissa. *Jean Després: Bijoutier et orfèvre entre Art déco et modernité.* Paris: Norma, 2009.

GLORIEUX, Guillaume. *Les Arts joailliers: Métiers d'excellence.* Paris: Gallimard/L'École des Arts Joailliers, 2019.

DE JOUVENEL, Anne. *Fred joaillier: De la rue Royale à la place Vendôme.* Paris: Les Éditions du Mécène, 1999.

JULIA DE FONTENELLE, Jean-Sébastien-Eugène, and François MALEPEYRE. *Nouveau manuel complet du bijoutier-joaillier et du sertisseur.* Paris: L. Mulo, 1927.

JUTHEAU DE WITT, Viviane. *Sterlé joaillier Paris.* Paris: Vecteurs, 1990.

LOYRETTE, Henri, ed. *Chaumet: Parisian Jeweler Since 1780.* Translated by Deke Dusinberre and Alexandra Keens. Paris: Flammarion, 2017.

MAURIES, Patrick. *Les Bijoux de Chanel.* Paris: La Martinière, 2012.

MEYER-STABLEY, Bertrand, and Laurence CATINOT-CROST. *Joailliers de légende: De Chaumet à Van Cleef & Arpels.* Paris: Bartillat, 2020.

MEYLAN, Vincent. *Archives secrètes Boucheron.* Paris: Télémaque, 2009.

———. *Mellerio dits Meller: Joaillier des reines.* Paris: Télémaque, 2013.

———. *Trésors et légendes: Van Cleef & Arpels.* Paris: Télémaque, 2012.

MOUILLEFARINE, Laurence, and Véronique RISTELHUERBER. *Raymond Templier: Le bijou modern.* Paris: Norma, 2005.

NADELHOFFER, Hans. *Cartier.* Paris: Éditions du Regard, 1984.

NERET, Gilles. *Boucheron: Histoire d'une dynastie de joailliers.* Paris: Pont Royal, 1988.

———. *Boucheron: Le joaillier du temps.* Paris: Conti, 1992.

RAULET, Sylvie. *Van Cleef & Arpels.* Paris: Assouline, 1997.

———, and Olivier BAROIN. *Suzanne Belperron.* Paris: La Bibliothèque des Arts, 2011.

RICHARD, Jean-Jacques. *Georges Le Turcq.* Paris: BoD, 2015.

———. *L'Histoire des Van Cleef et des Arpels.* Paris: BoD, 2014.

SAMET, Janie. *Chaumet.* Paris: Assouline, 2000.

SCARISBRICK, Diana. *Chaumet: Master Jewellers Since 1780.* Paris: Alain de Gourcuff, 1995.

SNOWMAN, A. Kenneth. *The Master Jewelers.* London: Thames & Hudson, 1990.

TRETIACK, Philippe. *Cartier.* Paris: Assouline, 1996.

VERLEYE, Léon. *Le Bijoutier à l'établi.* Paris: Desforges, Girardot et Cie, 1930.

Exhibition catalogs

L'ÉCOLE DES ARTS JOAILLIERS, with the support of Van Cleef & Arpels. *Lacloche joailliers, 1892-1967.* Paris: Norma, 2019.

INSTITUT DE FRANCE, MUSÉE JACQUEMART-ANDRÉ. *Boucheron, 130 années de création et d'émotion.* Paris: Boucheron, 1988.

INSTITUT DE FRANCE, MUSÉE DU PETIT PALAIS. *L'Art de Cartier.* Paris: Cartier, 1989.

MUSÉE DES ARTS DÉCORATIFS. *Van Cleef & Arpels: L'art de la haute joaillerie.* Paris: Les Arts Décoratifs, 2012.

MUSÉE DES ARTS DÉCORATIFS. *Cartier: Le style et l'histoire.* Paris: Réunion des Musées Nationaux, 2013.

MUSÉE DE LA MODE ET DU COSTUME. *Van Cleef & Arpels.* Paris: Paris-Musées, 1992.

MUSÉE D'ORSAY. *Mellerio, le joaillier du second Empire.* Paris: Réunion des Musées Nationaux, 2016.

**Practical Advice: Appraisal and Valuation,
Buying, Selling, Insurance**

ARAX, Jacques. *Le Guide pratique des bijoux et des pierres précieuses.*
Paris: Sand, 1988.

BEDEL, Catherine. *L'Argus des bijoux anciens.* Paris: Belfond, 1980.

CAILLES, Françoise. *Le Prix des bijoux.* Paris: ACR, 1989.

DARYS, Katherine and Michèle COHEN. *Le Guide de vos bijoux.* Paris: MA
Éditions, 1990.

MAZLOUM, Claude. *Bijoux et pierres: Les acheter et les vendre.* Antwerp:
Fiorimex, 1988.

————. *Choisir, acheter, offrir et porter les bijoux et les pierres précieuses.*
Rome: Gremese, 1991.

Photographic Credits

Front cover Art nouveau pendant necklace by René Lalique, in peridot, diamond, enamel, and glass © Neil Bicknell / Christie's Images / Bridgeman Images

Back cover and p. 26 Brooch designed by Massé, Boucheron jeweler, Musée des Arts Décoratifs, Paris © MAD, Paris

p. 4 *Le Bijou* © Maison Riondet

p. 10 *La Mode illustrée* © Maison Riondet

p. 12 *Princesse de Broglie* by Ingres, The Metropolitan Museum of Art, New York (NY), United States © The Metropolitan Museum of Art, Dist. RMN-Grand Palais/image of the MMA

p. 14 Gold and carnelian parure, Musée des Arts Décoratifs, Paris © MAD, Paris

p. 15 Portrait medallion, Châteaux de Malmaison et Bois-Préau, Rueil-Malmaison, © RMN-Grand Palais (Musée National des Châteaux de Malmaison et Bois-Préau)/ Gérard Blot

p. 16 Gold and citrine parure © Christie's Images/Bridgeman Images

p. 17 Bracelet with two women and vinaigrette, Musée des Arts Décoratifs, Paris © MAD, Paris

p. 19 *Marie-Caroline, Princess of Bourbon-Two Sicilies, Duchess of Berry*, by Guérin, Châteaux de Versailles et de Trianon, Versailles © RMN Grand Palais (Château de Versailles)/image RMN-GP

p. 20 Brooch © Maison Riondet/ Photographer Andreas Stenger

p. 21 Bracelet © Maison Riondet/ Photographer Andreas Stenger

p. 22 Necklace © Christie's Images/ Bridgeman Images

p. 23 Brooch © Christie's Images/ Bridgeman Images

p. 24 Vever pendant © Christie's Images/Bridgeman Images

p. 25 Lalique ring © Aguttes

p. 27 Ring © Maison Riondet/ Photographer Andreas Stenger

p. 29 Van Cleef & Arpels sautoir © Christie's Images/Bridgeman Images

p. 30 Mauboussin brooch © Sotheby's, New York, May 2012

p. 31 Bracelet and earrings © Christie's Images/Bridgeman Images

p. 32 Necklace and clips © Sotheby's, New York, Lot 259, February 2017

p. 33 Serlé brooch © Christie's Images/Bridgeman Images

p. 34 *Le Bijou* © Maison Riondet

p. 37 Tank bracelets © Maison Riondet/Photographer Andreas Stenger

p. 40 Sketch for necklace © Maison Riondet

p. 42 Després ring © Aguttes

p. 45 Berlin iron tiara © Christie's Images/Bridgeman Images

p. 46 *Fantaisies décoratives* © Maison Riondet

p. 48 Bracelet, Musée des Arts Décoratifs, Paris © MAD, Paris/ Jean Tholance

p. 49 Necklace © Maison Riondet/ Photographer Andreas Stenger

p. 50 *Les Pierres précieuses et les principaux ornements* © Maison Riondet

p. 53 Medallion-brooch with cameo, Château de Compiègne © RMN-Grand Palais (Domaine de Compiègne)/Thierry Le Mage

p. 54 Necklace © Maison Riondet

p. 55 Sterlé ring © Christie's Images/ Bridgeman Images

p. 56 Boucheron dress clip © Artcurial/Laurent Legendre for Studio Sebert

p. 57 Bracelet, Musée des Arts Décoratifs, Paris © MAD, Paris/ Jean Tholance

p. 58 Fouquet necklace © Artcurial/ Laurent Legendre for Studio Sebert © Adagp, Paris, 2024

p. 60 "Diamond," *L'Encyclopédie Larousse*, 1933 © Maison Riondet

p. 61 Ring © Maison Riondet/ Photographer Andreas Stenger

p. 62 Froment-Meurice comb, Musée des Arts Décoratifs, Paris © MAD, Paris/Jean Tholance

p. 63 Necklace © Christie's Images/ Bridgeman Images

p. 64 Earrings © Maison Riondet

p. 65 Poésie pendant designed by Grasset, Vever jeweler, Musée des Arts Décoratifs, Paris © MAD, Paris/ Jean Tholance

p. 66 Cartier brooch, © Christie's Images/Bridgeman Images

p. 67 Necklace, Musée des Arts Décoratifs, Paris © MAD, Paris/ Jean Tholance

p. 68 Fontenay earrings, Musée des Arts Décoratifs, Paris © MAD, Paris/ Jean Tholance

p. 69 Pendant © Maison Riondet

p. 70 Ring © Maison Riondet/ Photographer Andreas Stenger

p. 71 Large ear clips © Aguttes

p. 73 Dusausoy catalog © Maison Riondet

p. 74 Belperron ring © Aguttes

p. 75 Pair of bracelets © Christie's Images/Bridgeman Images

p. 76 *Le Bijou* © Maison Riondet

p. 78 Ring © Maison Riondet

p. 80 Rings © Maison Riondet/ Photographer Andreas Stenger

p. 83 Earrings © Maison Riondet/ Photographer Andreas Stenger

p. 84 Pair of bracelets © Sotheby's, Geneva, Lot 487, May 2015

p. 89 Cartier brooch © Christie's Images/Bridgeman Images

p. 90 Van Cleef & Arpels Zip necklace © Christie's Images/Bridgeman Images

p. 94 Lalique pendant necklace, Musée d'Orsay, Paris © RMN-Grand Palais (Musée d'Orsay)/Hervé Lewandowski

p. 96 Wing Aigrette tiara created by Joseph Chaumet for Gertrude Vanderbilt Whitney, 1910; platinum, diamonds, enamel; Collections Chaumet, Paris © Nils Herrmann

p. 98 Van Cleef & Arpels advertisement, illustrated by René-Sim Lacaze, Archives Van Cleef & Arpels © Van Cleef & Arpels SA

p. 100 Boucheron advertisement, illustrated by Pierre Simon © Adagp, Paris, 2024

p. 104 "Chaumet, Place Vendôme No. 12," 1920; preparatory sketch for an advertisement, featuring tiaras and diadems worn "*à la Joséphine*"; charcoal, gouache, and India ink on tracing paper; H. 30¼ × L. 21¾ in. (H. 77 × L. 55.5 cm); Collections Chaumet, Paris

p. 109 Jewelry, plate from *L'Illustration* © Maison Riondet including Fouquet and Sandoz © Adagp, Paris, 2024

p. 112 Vever jewelry, plate from *Journal des dames et des modes, Costumes parisiens* © Maison Riondet

p. 116 *La Pandore* © Maison Riondet

 **Institut National de Gemmologie**

Following the creation of the Association Française de Gemmologie in 1962, professionals and researchers founded the Institut National de Gemmologie (ING), a private technical college, in 1967 to train future gemologists and enable professionals to update and broaden their knowledge and skills.

Over the last half-century, the Institut has developed an internationally recognized training program, with a range of courses covering the spectrum of specializations in gemology and the luxury sector, particularly in relation to the jewelry and watchmaking industries. The ING is the leading training center for the gemology professions, and offers students a bachelor's degree program in gemology (Bachelor Gemmologue Expert), as well as courses aimed at professionals, amateur gemologists, and novices.

As a vocational and professional training center specialized in the study of gemstones and their uses, particularly in the field of jewelry and fine crafts, the Institut follows developments in its market closely and adapts its courses to match the needs of the sector.

Each year, the Institut adds to its impressive gemstone collection of more than 27,000 pieces, adapts its analysis tools and laboratories to keep pace with changing technologies, develops its learning methods, and introduces new subjects in its courses.

The ING works closely with the Association Française de Gemmologie and maintains relations with the companies operating in the sector. It is also a member of the Federation for European Education in Gemmology (FEEG) along with twelve other training centers in Germany, Spain, Portugal, Italy, Bahrein, and elsewhere. In collaboration with these establishments, the Institut National de Gemmologie has developed a system of competency evaluation for the European Gemmologist international diploma, for which it is an official examination center.

Its specialized bachelor's degree—a three-year undergraduate program—leads to the "Gemmologue Expert" certification, registered as a Level 6 qualification in the Répertoire National des Certifications Professionnelles (RNCP) under the number 35855 by decision of the director of France Compétences on September 15, 2021. It offers a new educational framework for passionate students seeking to acquire technical proficiency in gemstone identification, as well as a broader knowledge of markets, commercialization, trade, and geopolitics.

The Institut offers specialist courses, covering subjects that are constantly evolving to best meet the needs of professionals, in white diamond and colored diamonds, pearls, jewelry appraisal, and related techniques (stone design, CAD, etc.).

For the benefit of the jewelry and watchmaking industries and, more broadly, of the luxury sector, the ING has developed with the École Supérieure Technique en Art et Communication (EAC, a school dedicated to careers in the culture, luxury and art market sectors) a comprehensive master's degree course in luxury management.

 ING

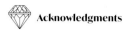

Acknowledgments

We wish, first of all, to thank the Institut National de Gemmologie (AD Éducation group) and, in particular, Lynda Degouve de Nuncques for her invaluable support from the start of the project, Charlotte Carrard, Mélanie Viala, and Martin Coriat. We extend our thanks to the school's students, whose many questions motivated, to no small degree, the writing of this book.

We are particularly grateful to Victoire de Castellane for her wonderful foreword.

We express our heartfelt thanks to all those who contributed to the illustrations of this book, namely Évelyne Possémé (Musée des Arts Décoratifs), Violaine d'Astorg (Christie's), Magali Teisseire (Sotheby's), Philippine Dupré la Tour (Aguttes), Julie Valade (Artcurial), Claire de Truchis Lauriston (Boucheron), Solène Taquet (Van Cleef & Arpels), Jean-Marc Mansvelt (Chaumet), Benoit Repellin (Phillips), and Andreas Stenger, who took many of the photographs of the jewelry pieces.

Our sincere thanks also go to Flammarion, and in particular to Virginie Maubourguet, Emmanuelle Rolland, and Henri Julien for their collaboration throughout this project.

We are grateful to the experts, jewelry dealers, gemologists, curators, teachers, and collectors, among others, who have, in one way or another, contributed to this work: Pascal Aronin, Olivier Baroin, Jean-Pascal Beaune, Maryse Béraudias, Bernard and Philippe Bouisset, Delphine Chabert (Genève Enchères), Guillaume Choumil, François Farges (Muséum National d'Histoire Naturelle de Paris), Renaud Fonverne, Jean-Claude Frediani, Guillaume Glorieux (L'École des Arts Joailliers), Jean-Pierre Guilhem, Béatrice Maisonneuve, Geneviève Mély, Guilhem Merolle (Collectissim), Fabian de Montjoye, Laurence Mouillefarine, Cédric Mure, François Planet (Musée des Beaux-Arts de Lyon), Jean-Jacques Richard, Olivier Segura (L'École des Arts Joailliers), Louis de Suremain, Raphaël Tuhdarian Vendome, Charlotte Wannebroucq, and Pierre Weber.

Finally, we owe a debt of gratitude to our families and friends for their precious support and endless patience.